From Stress to Success: Strategies for Profitable Properties Management

....

Mastering the Art of Property Management for Wealth Creation and Transform Your Rentals into Lucrative Investments.

●

LARRY HOWTON

CONTENTS

Introduction

The term "landlord" might be too strong of a word for many people out there. Many people see landlords as shady money-grabbing individuals that are only interested in maximizing their profits and harming the tenants.

However, this is not true because landlords go through a lot of pains and struggle to manage their property. I hope to change that perception by tenants and provide a guide on how to fight the stress and be the most successful landlord you can be.

I've spent a lot of time studying and investing in the real estate market, and I can tell you that it's a lot more complicated than most people think. Not only are you dealing with a complex legal system for tenants and landlords, but a lot of different factors outside of your control can continually put you under tremendous pressure.

Not only do landlords have to deal with tenants, but they also have to manage the property themselves. Some landlords do not have the right skills to manage the property, and it becomes a huge burden. Not only are they responsible for taking care of the property, but they are also responsible for finding good tenants, dealing with tenant needs and expectations, and managing any possible evictions.

While some people enter into real estate investing as a way of making more money from their investments, there is a lot of psychology behind it as well. Real estate investors are some of the most risk-tolerant individuals out there.

This is among the main reasons why many people tend to gravitate towards real estate investing. They want a way to make passive income, but they also want a way where they can control their own destiny. They believe that by taking the risk of becoming landlords, they will have a better chance of making a profit in the long run.

Starting to interact with tenants from the beginning can be a little intimidating. You are not only responsible for the actual property and ensuring that it is maintained, but you are also responsible for your tenants. If there is anything that I could put into this book, it has to be how to properly screen tenants and choose great tenants. This can often be one of the most difficult parts of being a landlord, especially in areas where rent prices are rising.

It is actually worth it if it helps you avoid any pitfalls with your property. Not only are you improving the property value, but you are also earning great returns on your investments. It can allow you to take advantage of the rising rental prices in certain markets for a longer period of time.

The most important thing landlords need to understand is

that there will always be something wrong with their properties at some point. Something will go wrong with the property, whether it is a leaking roof or a malfunctioning washing machine. You should be prepared for when these problems arise, so you can fix them quickly and efficiently.

Many landlords are not making any money because they are mismanaging their properties. In order to successfully manage your properties and make them profitable, it will take hours upon hours of hard work and dedication.

If you are not willing to put in the time and effort to make your properties profitable, then you might want to consider a different investment. If a landlord is unable to deal with the stress of owning rental properties, then they might be better off selling their properties and investing in other options.

While landlords can make great returns on their investments, there are also sometimes hidden costs that they are unaware of at the beginning. You may add value to your homes in a variety of ways other than simply renting them out. This is something that most landlords understand well. However, it is not something that everyone understands, and you might want to consider these options so you can maximize your profits later on down the road.

This book is a useful tool for landlords or any individual aspiring to be a landlord because it shares a wealth of knowledge from people with experience in the field. It is a well-known fact that firsthand experience is unbeatable.

Larry Howton is determined to give financial freedom to everyone, one person at a time. It's a financial brand with like-minded people who want to be successful financially. We teach people how to invest their way to financial success, assisting them in achieving financial success and building generational wealth. Larry Howton has made significant investments in a variety of industries, including retail, publishing, and market research. We want to ensure that everyone, young and old, has the same financial security that we enjoy.

Larry Howton is an authority in real estate investing because we have invested in many homes, and it is something we love. We have done extensive work on rental property maintenance, and we are eager to share them in this book.

Helping you achieve rental property success matters deeply to me because what you're about to learn has been proven accurate by experts.

Chapter 1:

Pursuing Excellence; Why Most Landlords Fail

There are many different ways to be a landlord — some landlords hire property managers who can handle the day-to-day operations of the property; others have good management skills and can spend a lot more time making sure their properties are running smoothly. Some landlords like their tenants and work with them throughout the year to maintain good relationships; others prefer not to interact with them at all until they receive rent payments.

Some landlords have a long list of properties and are very successful; others have a few properties and struggle to make ends meet. Some landlords purchase or develop property every year, creating wealth for themselves and financial freedom; others own one or two properties for years and never increase their number of holdings or their cash flow.

While there are many different ways to be a landlord, there is one thing that nearly all of them have in common: Most landlords are terrible at running their properties.

The reason most landlords fail has nothing to do with their intelligence or ability and everything to do with their ignorance. They don't know what they don't know. They are misinformed.

A landlord can be a smart man who has invested in the property but is overwhelmed by the property's responsibilities and the day-to-day issues that come with owning rental units, including conflict with tenants, maintenance issues, and messy finances. The landlord has hired a business manager to handle the day-to-day functions of owning properties, but those functions aren't being handled properly. This chapter will essentially give you tips on what makes a landlord successful and what are the main causes of failure.

Reasons why landlords fail

For you to become a successful landlord, you need to have a lot of knowledge in the field. Lack of understanding of the different aspects of this field can be a cause of major problems for you. Reasons for landlord failure are listed below.

Setting policies that discriminate against families: There are many different ways to govern a property. Some landlords set policies that prohibit families from having children in their properties; others don't allow large families or pets to live in their properties. Setting discrimination policies against families is one of the worst ways to fail as a landlord: It damages the property's reputation and makes it harder for any landlord who wants to rent to a family. It also costs landlords time and money because they have to dispute each demand of discrimination from tenants and take care of lawsuits when their tenants file them against the landlord. I have never heard of a discrimination policy that worked out well for landlords. The reason is obvious: Discrimination policies are unfair and work against the rights of families who want to live on a property.

Failing to keep promises made to tenants: Most landlords promise to provide certain things to their tenants when they sign a lease. If any of these promises aren't kept, it could lead to trouble. Things like pest control, air conditioning systems, or other amenities promised should be provided in full if they're promised. If a landlord doesn't keep their promises, the tenants will be upset and will feel like they've been lied to — and rightfully so.

Tenants want security knowing that their landlords are people of their word; without that trust between the two parties, there will be problems. If a landlord doesn't keep his promises and tenants feel like they've been lied to, no tenant will want to re-sign that lease.

Using security deposits for the wrong purpose: A security deposit is supposed to protect the landlord in case of damages or loss to the building. That doesn't mean that a security deposit should be used to pay for repairs, maintenance costs, or normal wear and tear unless they are authorized. If a landlord uses a security deposit for any other reason besides protecting themselves in case of damages to his property, he could be sued and lose the money.

Not keeping properties in good condition: Many landlords have run their properties for many years, and the buildings are in poor condition. They are unsure of what to do and feel overwhelmed by the responsibilities of property management. The buildings aren't maintained well enough, or not at all, so tenants complain about problems with lighting or bugs that make their lives unpleasant. The landlord doesn't have time to deal with maintenance issues because they are too busy dealing with tenants' issues instead of their own. Landlords who don't know how to keep their properties in good condition are not smart business people; they're just not doing their job.

Failing to understand the housing regulations: Many landlords are not aware of the housing laws that govern their properties. They don't know how to get around the rules, or they don't realize they need to. They expect that because they are a landlord, they don't have to follow the same rules as a homeowner in a home or apartment building. It's one thing for a homeowner not to follow the rules; it's another thing entirely for a property owner who knows how important rules and regulations are.

Not keeping up with the legal and zoning requirements: Most landlords are not aware of their legal and zoning requirements. They think they don't have to prepare for inspections and that they aren't legally required to have a property manager oversee the day-to- day operations of the property. Many landlords assume they can get away with not filing tax returns, collecting taxes, setting up bank accounts, getting insurance, or paying wages, and many think that because they don't follow these tasks out of laziness or ignorance, it doesn't matter.

Not paying attention to their financial information: Many landlords spend so much time dealing with the day-to-day problem of running the property that they don't take the time to understand their finances. They don't look at statements, and if they do, they don't understand what is happening with their finances. Rent collections are not managed properly; tenants are billed late and often, and payments are made after they've been due. The landlord doesn't know how much money is coming in and going out of the property and what their financial information looks like. Without this knowledge, landlords are not always aware of the state of their finances, which can lead to more money problems.

Violating tenants' right to privacy: Most landlords collect information, including social security numbers, IDs, and all the other necessary information that it takes to run a credit report on the tenants who want to live on their property. Although this is legal for a landlord to do, many fail to follow the rules of tenant privacy. They ask for too much information from the tenants; they run credit reports without permission from tenants, and they don't keep tenants' information confidential. All of these actions alone can lead to tenants having problems obtaining a loan or credit card since financial institutions do look at landlords' reports when they decide whether or not to approve or deny a tenant's application.

Not providing enough information about a property to tenants: Many landlords aren't responsible enough to provide their tenants with enough information about the property they're renting before signing a lease. If a landlord doesn't provide tenants with enough information, it will lead to confusion and disagreement with their tenants. Tenants need to know what they're getting themselves into when they sign the lease. The landlord must be ready to answer all their tenant's questions and provide them with detailed information on the property. If a landlord doesn't provide his tenant with the information he needs before signing a lease, he could lose that potential tenant and also hurt the reputation of his property as well.

Not paying the landlord's portion of property taxes: If you're a landlord, paying property taxes is one of your responsibilities. Even if you're not a landlord, you should still pay the property taxes. If landlords don't pay their portion of the property taxes, they could set a bad example for the tenants who will want to pay their portion of the property tax in order to help the landlord out. A potential tenant would feel like she or he was being taken advantage of. Also, if the tax collector or another agency comes to collect the taxes and a landlord hasn't paid his portion, the sheriff will most likely be called to seize the property. If a landlord doesn't pay their property taxes, it could cause them many problems that could lead to them going out of business.

Not maintaining appliances that tenants use: Keeping an appliance in good condition is a landlord's responsibility. If a landlord doesn't maintain the appliances, tenants will be frustrated, and it will cause problems for the landlord. Tenants have to pay a reasonable amount for rent, which basically means that they should expect that their landlord is living in the same conditions as well. If a landlord doesn't maintain his property, tenants get disappointed because they feel like they're paying for someone's laziness or not making their apartments as nice as expected. It causes problems between the two parties and could lead to eviction if the situation isn't handled properly.

Missing scheduled inspections: Inspections are necessary to make sure that properties are in good condition for tenants. If a landlord misses a scheduled inspection, they could set a poor example for their tenants. It could also cost them money. The longer past due an inspection is, the more the landlord will end up paying in fines. If the landlord doesn't perform their inspections, it could lead to some problems with the tenants as well. It would be considered unprofessional and make the tenant feel like there's not enough security or maintenance work being done on their property.

Not providing basic services such as snow removal services: Snow removal is an expense that landlords should have to pay during the winter season. The extra time and effort required to clear snow off of a property can take away from other duties, so it's crucial that landlords provide snow removal services for their tenants. If a landlord doesn't provide snow removal services, he could cause a problem with his tenants. Tenants will feel like the landlord is not taking their problems seriously because the snow removal isn't happening on time. It can also cause problems for the landlord and lead to them losing tenants who are irritated about the snow removal problem.

Not taking care of pest problems: Pest problems can be serious issues that will lead to more money being spent on bills because of the damage they do. If a landlord doesn't take care of pest problems, it could cause some serious damage to their property as well as expensive business bills that they need to pay. If an exterminator is called out and there are no pest problems, a bill will end up being sent to the landlord for professional exterminator fees. There could be other repercussions as well. If a landlord doesn't handle pest problems, it may cause them problems with the tenants as well. It may cause some tenants to move out of their apartments or to get angry and get the law involved.

Not re-renting properties on time: If a landlord does not rent his properties on time, the property will become vacant, and this could lead to problems for the landlord. Once a property gets vacant, it can cause even more problems for landlords who have many properties that are empty nearby. A vacant property can be a huge indicator of a problem. It could lose the landlord's potential tenants as well as possible customers and employees who live in the area. Ultimately, a landlord needs to be able to rent out his properties quickly in order to keep them occupied.

Not being willing to negotiate: Negotiating is one of the most important things that landlords need to do when renting out their properties. If a landlord doesn't negotiate properly and there are issues between them and a tenant, he could end up in serious trouble. The tenant will feel like the landlord isn't negotiating in good faith and will feel entitled to have their way due to the landlord making an offer that's below what is fair for both parties. It may also end up costing them money if they end up losing their property.

Common mistakes inexperienced landlords make

As a landlord, you can build a solid foundation for your business, but you have to make sure that you are aware of all the laws and procedures required so you do not get in trouble with your tenants or the courts.

Inexperienced landlords make a ton of mistakes; the ones below are the most common.

Failing to give proper notice before eviction: If you want to evict a tenant, you must provide them with proper notice. The notice is based on the term of the lease; for example, if the lease was for six months, then you need to provide them with a six months notice. Remember that even if your tenants have broken the law and it is illegal for them to live there, you still have to give them 30 days notice in order for them to move out. Otherwise, they will go to court and sue you for unlawful detainer, and you will have to pay for legal expenses. However, if your tenant refuses to move out, then you can ask the court to give you a possession order.

Failing to do proper tenant screening: If you decide to rent out a property, then you need to do proper tenant screening. It is your obligation as a landlord to ensure that the tenants are trustworthy. You want to find tenants who are not going to fail your property or misrepresent themselves. This is why proper tenant screening is so important; you want responsible tenants who pay their bills as well as tend to dry rot and prevent break-ins. You can partner with other landlords in the area or hire an agency that offers this service.

Assuming the property will always be rented: If you think that your property will always be rented, then this is an error that inexperienced landlords make all the time. However, if you want to build a solid rental business, then you need to make sure that the turnover rate of your properties does not exceed 20%. Most of the houses for rent and apartments for rent in the area will have a vacancy rate of 10%-20%, so you need to be aware of this.

Viewing the business as a hobby: Many landlords get into the business thinking that it will be like a hobby. However, if you want to make it a full-time business, then you have to treat your rental property as a business. You need to get your finances together and make sure that you are making enough money through the rent in order to live off of the profits. You need to remember that as a landlord, you will be responsible for all the repairs made on the property, so it is important that you charge fair fees. However, if you are looking for a way to get tenants into your property without having to worry about the rent, you need to consider finding a tenant management company in the area.

Not keeping records: In order to keep the tenants happy, you need to keep complete and accurate records of everything happening in your buildings on a regular basis. This will include making sure that all occupants have proper identification, as well as paying any late rent or for damages that were caused during the time that they lived in your building. You should make sure that all of this information is being taken care of and kept in one location. The first thing you want to do is create a system for recording all of your tenant information and then follow it every single day.

Hiring an inexperienced property manager: Some landlords do not have time to manage the property, and so they find a property manager to take care of everything for them. However, there are many inexperienced property managers who could potentially get you in trouble with the law. You need to be careful since some people will begin deducting things that they are not supposed to in order to make more money. For example, if you tell them not to charge some services, then they will do so anyway and pocket the money. If you want to hire a reliable property manager, then you need to go through several interviews before hiring someone; otherwise, you might end up getting sued by tenants who are being charged illegal fees.

Hiring family members to manage your property: Even if you have worked with your family before, you still need to make sure that they are up to the task. If you hire a family member, they might not treat the property in the same manner as you would. This could result in problems in the future. In fact, if family members are on the property management team, it is easier for them to alter and remove records. This makes it difficult for auditing companies to determine what has been done on the property. To avoid this kind of problem, make sure that whoever is managing your rental property has a great deal of experience in this field.

Not being available for emergencies: It comes with being a landlord; there will always be emergencies to deal with at some point in time. You should have a plan for handling emergencies if you want to be a good landlord. Make sure that you have the contact information of other local landlords, as well as several maintenance workers and electricians on your phone. You will also want to make sure that you have a good relationship with your tenants as well because they will be the ones who can help you with any kind of emergency that might arise.

Not having a current insurance policy: It is important that you are covered by insurance in case anything happens in the property. You need to check your policy to make sure that it is still up-to-date. Also, you need to make sure that all of the tenants are listed on your policy because if they are not, then it will not cover them if there are damages caused by your tenant. If a tenant vacates the property and has damaged it, then how will you cover these repairs if you do not have full coverage?

Not maintaining a clean property: As a landlord, you want to keep the property in pristine condition. You need to pay for regular maintenance and make sure that it does not look like a dump. However, some landlords think that they can cut corners in order to save money, but this is not a good idea. If your tenant is living in an apartment that looks like it is falling apart, then they will start looking for another place to live. This means you will have to spend time and money finding new tenants, which might lead to you losing money if you cannot find anyone else willing to pay rent on your property. Make sure that you are doing everything in your power to provide a safe, clean property that is well-maintained.

Failing to know the legal procedure: It is important that you know your legal procedure as a landlord. If you do not, then you could get in trouble for breaking the law. For example, if you fail to fix something in the property and it catches on fire and damages another tenant's property, then you might be sued by this other tenant if their "stuff" was damaged in any way. It is always important that you know what your responsibilities are, such as knowing how long notice must be given for tenants to leave. A lawyer will be able to guide you through this process.

Not obtaining permissions for renovations: If you want to renovate the property, then you need to keep filling out forms until you get permission. However, the only way to know if your property will be approved is by making sure that all of the necessary paperwork is filled out and ready for inspection. If these documents are not ready, then your application will most likely be refused. Also, it is important that you make sure that all tenants agree with whatever new rules change as a result of this renovation. Do not make changes without knowing first if they are okay with them or not; otherwise, tenants will be able to sue you for violating their rights

Illegal tenants living in your unit: Sometimes, landlords do not know who their tenants are. If this happens in your building, then it is important that you contact the police. Make sure that you know how to spot if a person is illegal or not. There are certain things that illegal tenants will do to try and make you think that they are legal, such as having false identification or borrowing the identification of a family member who has legal status. If you follow the law and keep proper records of what is going on in your building, then you will be protected from any issues in the future

Not knowing when to get a lawyer involved: If you are not a landlord with experience, then it is best to have someone from the community who knows what they are doing to help review your lease and guide you in the right direction. When you do get a lawyer involved, make sure that you speak with one that is well known for their knowledge of rental properties law. Always ask them if you are unsure about a particular issue. If possible, go with an attorney that specializes in landlord law; otherwise, they will not be able to understand all of the different rental property laws and how they apply in your case.

Not having a good relationship with tenants: As mentioned earlier, you need to have a good rapport with your tenants. If they are not satisfied with how you are running the building and taking care of problems, then they could be more willing to move out before the lease is up and even tell other people about what is going on at your building. If you have problems with your tenants, then you will most likely find it difficult to work with them. As a landlord, this could get you into a lot of trouble in the future.

As an inexperienced landlord, you should learn as much as you can about being a landlord. This includes anything from learning how to properly fill out the lease agreement to how to deal with tenants who are causing problems. Avoid making these common mistakes, so you don't have any problems with your tenants or the courts.

The Essence of Renting

A lot of individuals and businesses get into renting because they believe that it is a passive and easy way to earn money. However, just like other forms of work, especially if you do it right, renting can be very profitable. In this part, we explain some of the advantages of doing a rental business and why you should consider starting.

It's a passive income source: When you rent an apartment out, you make money for a long time. Even if you stop renting out the property, you would have still: earned a good sum of money. It's like winning a lottery that never runs out of its winning numbers. One of the most important reasons why this business is great is because it offers a passive income source while not requiring much work. This was probably one thing that made many individuals and businesses consider entering this line of work. If you're looking for a way to make money on the side, this could be worth your time and effort.

Greater security compared to other forms of investment: Instead of putting your money in a stock market or mutual fund, you can be sure that your money is going to be safe with the rental business. You would have the assurance that no matter what happens, your money would still be there and earn you some interest annually.

There are so many stories of people losing their hard- earned money in the stock market or even in the real estate business because of factors beyond their control.

The ability to sell the property at the best possible price: One of the best things about this business is that you can still sell the property, just like when you buy a stock. You would have more control over when to sell and for how much. If you think that the price of real estate would be going higher, then you won't hesitate to sell your properties at a profit rather than letting them sit there. A broker can help with selling your properties if you don't want to do it or if you don't have time to do so. This way, you wouldn't have to worry about letting the properties sit there and become obsolete. You would still get a lot of profit even if you decide to sell them anytime.

It can help build your retirement income: If you are planning on retiring soon, then renting out your properties could be a great option for you. As long as the number of tenants is stable and the rent keeps increasing, it would make sense that you would be earning more in the future, especially if you have other properties too.

There are some people who prefer renting out their properties to tenants instead of living in them because they have other properties or houses that they can live in, and they would still earn a lot of money from the rent.

With this, it would be easier for them to save up for their retirement without worrying about overspending.

You can easily finance your property if you rent it out: If you need cash or if you have some properties that you want to purchase, it would be easier to get financing from your bank if you are already renting out your property. Your assets are already generating some passive income for as long as the tenants keep renting them, so it would be easier for the bank to see how much cash flow you have coming in. You can even borrow money from other companies such as peer-to-peer lending companies. If you live in a place that has a good rental market, you would be able to get financing easily.

You can still make money even if you don't live in that place: When you rent out a property, whether it is an apartment or house, you are guaranteed to make money. What if you live in another country or state and cannot be around the property every day? If you have hired a property manager to look after the place for you, then everything would still be okay. You can visit your properties once every quarter or even once a year to see how they are doing.

You can make even more profits by adding on value:
When you are already renting out an apartment or house, why not add on some value? You can create a small studio apartment, for example, inside your rented-out apartment or house so that you can rent it out as a separate unit. You can also expand your rental business by buying another property so that you can rent it out as well. This will provide you with better returns and make the investment safer.

Tax Benefits of Becoming a Landlord

Property taxes are due by April 15th, and it's important to stay on top of the tax bill, especially for landlords. The requirements for property taxes vary with each state, and some states have different dates. If you're a landlord, here are some tax advantages for your property:

Landlords get a mortgage interest deduction: This is the most common tax benefit property investors enjoy; by deducting interest from your mortgage, you are able to save money. The IRS allows you to deduct all of your mortgage interest if you use the loan for rental property. According to the IRS, this includes points paid upfront in addition to amortized points over the life of the mortgage. You can't deduct interest on investment properties until after a 12-month holding period.

Depreciation: When you buy a property, the first thing that comes to many people's minds is depreciation. The process of trading up, also known as depreciation, is a way to save money. By writing off the expense of your home over a number of years, it lowers the taxable income you make from renting out your property.

Property taxes relief: In 2015, the IRS reduced the standard deduction to $6,300 for single taxpayers (or married filing separately) and increased the personal exemption to $3,600 per person. If you are in a high tax bracket but own rental property, you may qualify for the personal exemption on your federal tax return. You can also get tax relief by renting out a vacant rental property. In most states, vacant or unused rental properties are not taxed; however, this is not always the case, and it's important to check with your local municipality before selling.

Sales tax deduction: Homeowners with primary residences and landlords who rent out a property can deduct the sales taxes they pay. Sales tax rates vary widely by state and county, but as a landlord, it's important you keep good records of what you spend on your rental property; otherwise, you won't be able to write it off.

You can deduct the cost of travel to your property: If you travel to the property in order to maintain or repair it, you may be able to deduct your expenses. You can deduct mileage based on IRS Form 4562. Deduct 57.5 each highway mile and 25 per other miles if your vehicle achieves fewer than 20 miles per gallon. If your vehicle gets more than 20 miles per gallon, deduct 54¢ per highway mile and 28¢ per other miles. You can't deduct the cost of driving your car to the job (unless you use a special vehicle that gets less than 10 miles per gallon, in which case you can deduct 80% of the vehicle's cost). The IRS also allows you to deduct gas and oil costs if you use your vehicle for work-related travel. You're not allowed to deduct personal travel, such as vacations or errands that have nothing to do with business.

There are tax savings when terminating a lease: If your tenant opts out of a lease early, you are able to keep some of your tax benefits even without collecting rent on a property. Here's how it works: If the tenant leaves before the end of the year, you can deduct $100 or 10% of your adjusted gross income, whichever is higher. You can also depreciate any improvements to the property that you didn't get to use. For example, if a tenant moved out after six months but you put in new brick in anticipation of a five-year lease, you can still depreciate that because you got six months' worth of wear out of it.

Legal Fees Deduction: If you've sued your tenant for unpaid rent, you can deduct those costs from your income. For example, if you own an apartment building and a tenant leaves owing rent and damages, you may have to go to court. The legal fees associated with the case are tax-deductible. If the tenant doesn't pay up or fix the property, then these deductions are allowed for any repairs or maintenance done to the property in order to get back some of your money.

Tax Credits: If you have a historic building that has been fully rehabbed, there is a 20% tax credit that could be applied toward some of the expenses - up to $5 million on properties that are 50 years or older. You can get a 10% credit for properties that are at least 20 years old, and you can get a 5% credit for properties that are at least 10 years old. You can only apply one credit toward a property, so it might make sense to put that 20% into your next project. Also, there is a 30% tax credit for rehabbing or restoring historic buildings - up to $20 million - if the rehabilitation takes place between 2009 and 2018. The appraisal requirement is 50% of the cost over $250,000 (or 50% of the eligible costs in excess of $100,000). You can apply for either or both tax credits if you're otherwise qualified.

Things great landlords do differently from normal ones.

Landlords have difficult jobs. They must be experts in the residential industry, and he or she must be able to keep up with today's complex rental market. These are some of the responsibilities that come with being a landlord, but luckily for landlords everywhere, there are plenty of things they can do to make their property stand out from all the rest. Great landlords have very many things in common with each other as well as do things differently from the average landlord. Some of these are explained below:

They know their numbers: A landlord who doesn't know his or her numbers is playing a dangerous game. It's impossible to avoid knowing certain details about your home and its financial position. Renting out property is an investment that requires a high level of knowledge and planning, coupled with understanding your finances. A good landlord knows exactly how much he or she can afford to pay to service loans every month, how much their property is actually worth, what insurance they should buy, how much they should put away for repairs and maintenance, etc.

Landlords who are successful know how to locate suitable rental homes: Once a landlord has the knowledge and the numbers, he or she must find the right rental properties. This is an important process that all landlords must go through in order to be successful in their endeavors; this is where things get tricky because finding good homes isn't always easy. It's easy if you know what to look for. If a property looks dark and dingy, has lots of trash lying around, or is overall run down, chances are you might want to look elsewhere. You may think this makes a good rule to follow, but it's not always accurate. A place that looks like it was never cleaned can be cleaned up with very little work; basically, you have to think about the long term.

They are aware of tax advantages: The state and federal tax codes can be very complicated at times, but as a landlord, you need to be able to read them and understand them in their entirety. There are several things you may do with your property to reduce your tax burden. For instance, if you leave your property vacant too long when the taxes are due, it's important to make sure that you save up for the taxes before they get due. This can help you in the long run, considering that one of the most important things a landlord can ever do is to make sure his property maintains a proper tax status.

They have a strict rental policy: You cannot have a good rental property without a strict rental policy. A landlord has to know what their tenants are getting into. This policy can be anything from the small things like smoking and drinking to the bigger ones like noise, pets, and criminal activity. One thing a landlord can do is to have an in-house lawyer who can handle everything for you that tends to come up during tenancy; this is just one of the many ways landlords can make their properties more successful.

They are there for their tenants: Good landlords will always be there for their tenants. If there is ever a problem that arises, they will help the tenant in any way possible. It's important to make sure it's a situation that can be handled at hand without having a major negative impact on the property as well. A landlord who isn't always at the property can lead to problems when it comes to paying rent and taking care of repairs as well. A good landlord is always on top of everything and takes the extra steps to make sure his tenants are satisfied.

They are understanding and respectful of the tenants' rights: A good landlord does not take advantage of his or her tenants; this is something else that differs from the average landlord. A good landlord understands that they have a responsibility as well as a lot of power to help their tenants achieve success in life. They understand that by facilitating a good relationship between their tenants and themselves, they can accomplish great things. This is also what makes a good landlord so successful.

You should let the tenant know that you are there if they ever have any problems, and if they do, it's your job to fix them as soon as possible.

Great landlords are always learning: To be successful in anything you do, it's important to always keep learning. A landlord needs to be very knowledgeable in his or her field. Knowing everything there is to know about the rental market and the industry, in general, can allow a landlord to make more informed decisions, as well as know when to make changes. This is something every landlord needs to work on and practice regularly. If a landlord always knows their numbers, understands tax advantages, has a strict rental policy, and understands the tenants' rights, they can never go wrong.

They always look for new investment opportunities: There are many things that can happen during the time when you're a landlord, but the risk should always be present. This is why an owner needs to be ready for anything; a good landlord never stops looking for new investment opportunities in order to make sure they do not go bankrupt. As a landlord, it's important to understand that risks always exist, and if you don't, your profit will go down too.

Principles of a great landlord

If you're a landlord, or someone looking for a rental home, it's a good idea to arm yourself with knowledge. There is more to being a landlord than just collecting rent from tenants and flipping properties as quickly as possible. Here are some of the key principles every landlord should adhere to.

Take your job as a landlord seriously: Being a landlord entails a great deal of responsibility. You will always be under pressure to make sure that things are running efficiently. You should put a lot of effort into what you do and ensure your tenants are well taken care of. This means showing up on time for property viewings and being prepared to walk through the property with prospective tenants. It also means showing up on time for rent collections and making sure you have all your documents in order, so you don't have to chase payments around.

Manage your property like a business: Always think of your property as a business. In other words, you should ensure that you treat it well for the sake of continued profit. You must ensure that you generate income from the property. Being a landlord means being an entrepreneur. If you want to make money, you're going to have to fill in the forms, manage receipts and get a financial statement. It's important for you to understand your expenses and keep track of them before they go out of business. This means tracking your mortgage or rental payments, as well as all other expenses. You should also monitor your property's value and make sure it doesn't drop.

Be mindful of fair housing: As a landlord, you should always be mindful of your role in ensuring equal opportunities for all of your tenants. This means making sure that you don't discriminate against any tenant based on their age, race, or sex. You don't have to be forthcoming about this, but it's important that you do the right thing at all times.

Understand your local municipality and state laws:
There are many laws that govern how you operate as a land-lord. For instance, it is against the law to discriminate against prospective tenants based on their race or gender. You should ensure that you aren't charging more than what is allowed in terms of rent. Your state and local government are excellent resources when it comes to understanding local laws.

Market your property thoroughly: You need to market your property thoroughly if you want to find good tenants for it. You can also use a broker if you don't have the time or skills to find tenants. In addition, you should also consider hiring a company that does thorough background checks on potential tenants. This will help you find anyone with a criminal record, which can be useful in ensuring the safety of other tenants on the property.

Pre-screen your tenants to eliminate troublemakers:
Your property will probably attract a lot of people over time. You need to check their credentials to make sure that they aren't going to be trouble for others. If you have a lot of bad tenants, this will also make it harder to find good ones in the future. To avoid that, you should consider waiting to see how a tenant rents out before deciding whether or not they can stay at the property.

Sign a solid lease: You'll also want to be certain that you don't have any legal difficulties with your lease. It is important to always have a written lease agreement that clearly spells out the tenant's responsibilities, as well as what they will be paying. This will ensure that you aren't going to be liable for their improper behavior.

Handle problems carefully: There will be problems now and then with your tenants, but you need to make sure that you handle them tactfully. It can be easy to evict a tenant on the spot, but this can be problematic if they aren't actually breaking any of the rules. When you're facing a tricky situation, always think things through and avoid doing something too drastic.

Be honest with your tenants: When it comes to managing your property, you should be as open and honest with your tenants as possible. You must be honest with them if they have any queries or problems.

Otherwise, they won't trust you, and this will create a lot of problems. You need to make sure that your tenants know that you'll always tell them the truth, even if it isn't convenient for you. Just remember that whatever it is that they ask you to do, it should be reasonable.

Have a system for dealing with contractors: You also need to have a system when it comes to contractors hiring out your property. They can be essential for improving the property in a very short period of time, but you need to make sure that you have a good system of contacting them and making sure that the work is done correctly. You should also always spell out what needs to happen for additional costs to be applied so that any potential issues can be dealt with quickly.

Chapter 2:

Bad Tenants Are Not Welcomed Here

Landlords use tenant screening to guarantee that they are renting to qualified and stable tenants. The world of tenant screening is a tricky one, and by no means is it easy to find good renters. But this doesn't mean that landlords should give up. There are many things you can do as a landlord to ensure that when you finally do find your next tenant, they really are the right one! Importance of Tenant Screening

A lot of people in our society believe that it is up to the landlord to conduct a tenant screening before agreeing to rent out a property. Most landlords and realtors are likely not aware of the importance of tenant screening and often only perform one type of screening, fingerprinting. Each state has different laws concerning what type of information is required for a landlord or agent, but in most cases, they need to know if the applicant has ever been arrested or convicted. Tenant screening is important because of the following reasons:

Tenant screening gives a landlord a competitive advantage: If a landlord or agent can find tenants that are mistake-free and have no history of criminal activity, it proves that the landlord is being responsible. This gives them an advantage over other landlords in the area because they will be able to rent out their property at a higher price for the same house. It also makes a great impression on other potential tenants. Since many people in our society look up to landlords, it gives them confidence in renting their house without any concerns about who will be living next door.

It saves time and money: Tenant screening saves time and money by allowing landlords to put potential tenants through the process that they need instead of accepting everyone. By rejecting the people that are not eligible, it will save both parties time and money because each party does not have to waste time in court because of a dispute. The landlord does not need to argue about something that could have been prevented with tenant screening.

It protects against fraudulent applicants: By performing tenant screening, you can protect yourself from being scammed by people who go through great effort before applying. If someone is going to go through so much trouble to get a property, it is best that you know who they are and what they are capable of. If a person does not have the intentions of maintaining their rental property, you will likely find this out before they end up in court. Tenant screening also protects against fraudulent applicants when someone who has a criminal history applies yet goes through all the trouble to fool the landlord. This can be done by doing up-to-date background checks on anyone that is applying for any type of property and by recording all documents sent to or received by any landlord.

It can help avoid eviction of tenants: Each year, landlords file for eviction of tenants because of unpaid rent. By performing tenant screening, it will help to avoid this. By being able to know the tenant before renting out a property, you can tell if they have the ability to pay the rent on time. If someone does not have a history of paying bills or has a bankruptcy or foreclosure on their record, you can deny their application and save yourself from future issues by evicting them when rent is not paid on time.

It increases tenant satisfaction: Tenant screening will allow the tenant to feel more comfortable in their rental home. If a tenant screening was performed on them, it would reassure them that they are with a responsible landlord and that the house is being taken care of. Proper tenant screening can help avoid problems between landlords and tenants in the future because it shows the effort is being made to keep both halves of the relationship happy.

Tenant Screening Process

Tenant screening typically consists of a three-step process:

Application

The application process is the first step in picking good tenants. A landlord should make sure that the application is detailed and thorough so that they can learn as much about the tenant as possible. They should ask questions about their job, their income, etc., but they should also ask questions that will identify if they might be a potential problem tenant later on. This can include asking if they have ever been evicted or if they have been written up at their last place. Landlords should also pick out what information they will require to verify information on the application. It is important to try to cover as many bases as possible with the application so that you won't later learn something that you didn't know when you decided to rent to them.

Credit Check

Landlords should have the tenant complete a credit check as part of the application process. Landlords should only use licensed and bonded credit bureaus for this purpose. A landlord should know whether or not an applicant has been denied credit in the past or if they are using any type of third-party source to get their background check done. This can include using services such as Fair Credit Reporting (FCR) or TransUnion, which are both private companies.

Criminal Background Check

Landlords should always check criminal backgrounds with the tenant. If the tenant has a criminal record, it will help you to determine if they are a good fit for your property. This can also help you avoid any discrimination lawsuits, which are becoming more and more common in today's society. The tenant should agree to this background check, and it should be included in the lease.

Tenant Screening Agencies

There are many different companies offering tenant screening services, but it is important to make sure that they have been properly licensed and bonded if they are conducting criminal background checks as part of their service. All United Property Management receives all of its tenant screening through Fingerprinting Companies, Inc. By getting tenant screening from this professional background check agency, we can be sure that the information is reliable and will not cause us any legal problems.

Understanding Tenant Screening Laws

One bad experience with a problematic tenant can make a landlord understand the importance of tenant screening laws. Tenant screening laws are often state and county-specific, so it's important to understand your local requirements.

According to HUD's website, the federal Fair Housing Act prohibits discrimination in rental housing based on: Race, Color, National Origin, Religion, Sex, Familial Status (families with children under 18), and Handicap (physical or mental disability). Potential tenants should therefore not be discriminated against based on the above factors.

A landlord must also make reasonable accommodations for tenants with disabilities. The Federal Fair Housing Act requires that landlords make reasonable accommodations to their rules, policies, and services in order to keep housing accessible.

A landlord can deny renting to anyone with a felony record. However, they cannot use generalizations against all felons. The landlord should ask the tenant whether they were convicted and not whether they were charged with a crime.

Landlords may only rely on negative information that is accurate, complete, and up-to-date when they are determining their initial decision to rent or lease to a potential tenant or applicant. This information could be gleaned from criminal background checks or credit checks. If a landlord requests credit reports, he should give the applicant written notice that can be used as proof of what information was given to the landlord. If the landlord misrepresents or fails to provide accurate and up- to-date information, then it could constitute a violation of fair housing law.

Landlords must keep a record of all tenant applications and applicants that they interview. This includes a copy of the application, all documented background information, and copies of the results of any credit checks or other background checks (to include any tenant screening fees paid for) for at least three years after the date that the landlord accepts an applicant or tenant.

Criminal background checks must be done by a licensed, bonded, and professional organization. A landlord can only use a background check from a professional background check agency if he has been obtained from his state. In the state of Texas, all of the information that's provided by the tenant screening company is then confidential for the landlord and cannot be purchased or used by anyone else. The tenant will also have to sign an agreement (usually found in their application) that they either agree or disagree on releasing this information in writing if they decide to move.

How to Avoid Discrimination Charges During the Tenant Screening Process

A landlord should avoid asking certain questions which may be discriminatory from the potential tenant's perspective. The following are examples of questions the landlord should avoid:

Do you have a disability?

This question is illegal to ask in some states. A landlord can only ask if a tenant requires any reasonable accommodations, which can include wheelchair ramps or doorways widened.

What race or national origin are you?

A landlord can only ask this question if they have complied with the federal Fair Housing Act and determined that they are accepting tenants based on their race, skin color, or national origin.

What is your religion?

This question may indicate the intent to discriminate based on religion. It is advisable for landlords to avoid asking it and accept tenants from all religions.

Are you gay?

A landlord should not discriminate on the basis of sexual orientation or gender identity. Some states do have housing discrimination protection laws that prohibit landlords from discriminating against LGBTQ people.

Are you married?

A landlord should not ask this question because the answer to it is irrelevant. Marital status may only be asked if it's related to their ability to pay rent or if their credit has been checked.

Do you have children?

A landlord should also not reject a tenant based on this information, although they may do so if they feel that the tenant's children may cause a problem in the building.

Questions a Landlord Can Legally Ask During the Tenant Screening Process

The American Civil Liberties Union published a list of questions landlords can legally ask during the tenant screening process in order to determine if an applicant is eligible for tenancy. A landlord is legally allowed to ask the following questions:

Ask about Tenant references: Landlords are legally allowed to ask a prospective tenant's references, although they must inform the tenant that their responses may be forwarded on to others. A landlord can give the tenant an opportunity to correct any false information provided in their reference but note that you cannot use them against them if you have already accepted them as a tenant and have plans to reject them.

Income information: If the potential tenant is applying for a long-term lease, landlords are legally allowed to ask for their income for at least 60 days before the potential tenant moves in. If the lease is for less than 60 days, you are allowed to ask about their current job and salary. You are also allowed to ask about the number of people living in the home and if any of them have children.

Criminal record of the tenant: Landlords are legally allowed to ask about the criminal record of the prospective tenant. Landlords can legally perform background checks on the prospective tenant using the information provided by the applicant, both of the previous landlord and of any other landlords with whom they have done business in the past year. Landlords can also ask a prospective tenant about criminal convictions that occurred in their state, as long as this information is provided in a statement signed under penalty of perjury.

Credit history: Landlords are legally allowed to ask about a prospective tenant's credit history. You may ask about the number of inquiries the potential tenant has had, their payment history, and if they currently owe money on a loan.

Check Tenant's employment history: A prospective tenant's employment history is used as one of the primary criteria landlords use in order to determine whether or not they are credit-worthy and responsible renters. It's also utilized to figure out how much rent they'll be able to pay. A landlord can ask prospective tenants questions about employment history, but the tenant cannot provide this information if they are currently employed or in the process of starting a new job.

Pets: Landlords can legally ask prospective tenants about their pets, even if they plan to live alone. A landlord cannot require a tenant to get rid of current animals before moving into the property, however. Landlords also cannot require them to get rid of their pets if they move out early or decide not to renew a lease once it has expired. A background check is legally required in order for landlords to learn whether or not they have violated any animal-related laws and whether or not they are considered a threat to other tenants at your property.

Ask about the length of time the tenant will be leasing the property: This is a reasonable question to ask because if your vacancy is for six months and your tenant only wants to lease for three months, you may need to find another tenant quickly. A landlord can also ask if their lease will be renewed at the end of the rental period. If you deny a renewal request from an established tenant, you are required by law to give them a termination notice prior to evicting them from your property.

Other people living in the applicant's home: Landlords are not allowed to discriminate against someone because of what other people in their household may do. A landlord can, however, ask an applicant if he or she is married and how many people live in the house. A landlord can also ask if there are any additional people applying for tenancy at the same time as the potential tenant.

Ask how much the tenant plans to pay for rent: A landlord is legally allowed to ask a prospective tenant about their current rent payment but cannot do so if a lease has already been signed. A landlord can also ask about the tenant's financial background, such as their credit score and current bank statement, for proof of income. These questions are important in order to determine whether or not a prospective tenant will be able to afford the monthly rent on your property when they move in.

Ask about their past rental payment history: Landlords are legally able to ask both a prospective tenant and their previous landlord whether or not they have paid their rent on time in the past. A tenant, however, does not need to provide any information about his or her past rental payments if there is an active lawsuit involving the previous landlord.

Past evictions: A landlord can legally ask the tenant applicant whether or not they have ever been evicted, but they cannot ask them the specific reason for their eviction. A tenant applicant can legally deny this information and then later have their previous landlord contact you. A landlord is still able to deny a tenant's application based on past evictions if there are any red flags in their rental history.

Building the ultimate tenant application form

The tenant application form is a crucial element in the screening process. Preparing a detailed tenant application form is important because it helps you gather as much information from the tenant as possible. The following are some of the basic components of a good tenant application form.

The applicant's contact information: This includes the applicant's name, email address, phone number, and an operator to contact if there is an emergency. This is the most important piece of information on the tenant application form because it will provide you with a way to reach the applicant without having to get things delayed by an email.

The apartment they are applying for: The information on the property should be detailed and include a clearly identifiable address, phone number, and mailbox, as well as a clear picture of what exactly the apartment looks like. In addition, you can include a general description of the apartment that includes things like the size of the kitchen and living room, number of bedrooms, type of neighborhood, and any other relevant information.

The landlord's contact information: The landlord should be clearly identified on the application, as well as a clear picture of what building or property they own. The landlord should have a separate section on the application where they can explain their qualifications and why they are qualified to rent to someone who is moving in.

The current and prior residence information: In the tenant application, where the applicant currently lives and where they previously lived is important. The information gleaned from these two sections will allow you to track an applicant's history and may help you avoid unwise renting decisions that could lead to a whole lot of problems down the line.

The application date: It can be useful in case there are any misunderstandings between the landlord and tenant later on. Many landlords prefer applications to come in on a predetermined date, but some are flexible. While you must be aware of any deadlines that may be set by the landlord, a good tenant application form will include a clear and up-to-date date for when applications should be submitted.

Employment History and Proof of Income: Another very important piece of information on an application is the applicant's current employment status. Landlords need assurance that the tenant is able to pay for rent and keep up with financial obligations in a timely manner. A good tenant application will include proof of income and possibly even copies of W-2 forms from the current employer as proof of where their money is coming from.

Authorization to Contact Prior Landlords, Employers, and Pull Credit and Criminal Histories: If the potential tenant does not fill out this section, it could be a sign that they have something to hide. If a prior landlord says that they will not provide information or otherwise refuses to cooperate with you, do not automatically assume that this means the tenant has bad credit or is of bad character. They may have had a disagreement with their landlord or had some kind of misunderstanding that has since been cleared up. Unless you have strong evidence to suggest otherwise, try not to assume the worst.

Chapter 3:

Holding on to Good Tenants

The best part about owning rental properties is that it's possible to make money without ever having to lift a finger. You can relax and watch your passive income rise as long as your tenants pay their rent on time and don't cause any problems. It is very important to relate well with your tenants, especially if they are good. This chapter will walk you through keeping a good tenant, mistakes to avoid, and building a good relationship with them.

Importance of Having a Good Relationship with Your Tenants

If you are looking to rent a property, it can be a nerve- wracking experience. Not only is there the whole question of finding the right place for you, but also securing it and having an amenable relationship with your tenant. Having a good relationship is a very important component that landlords should strive to achieve. Below are some of the benefits that come with having a good relationship with your tenants:

They'll want to rent from you again and even increase the lease duration: People are more likely to rent from you again if you're fair; keep your word and treat them well. If you relate well with your tenants, they will tell their friends about it and may even refer new tenants to you. If your tenants believe in the value of your service, then they will recommend you to others. It's much easier to attract good tenants if they know that they can trust you (and get rid of the bad ones without too many problems).

You'll make more money: You will make more money if you have a strong relationship with your tenants, and they stay for the long term. If a tenant stays in one of your properties for many years, they will pay you higher rent each month. For example, if your tenant currently pays $750 a month and they've been renting from you for three years, the rent has been increasing each year by around $25 per month. In this case, they'll be paying around $875 a month after another three years.

In the long term, there's a much higher chance that you can increase the rent each year if you have a good tenant. If you have tenants who create problems for you, both financially and personally, your chances of being able to increase your rent each year are much smaller. Therefore, it makes sense to try and keep good tenants over a period of time.

You save money because there are fewer vacant properties: A good relationship with your tenants helps attract more tenants through referrals. You don't want many empty properties in your portfolio because it costs money to maintain them. In fact, it costs more money to maintain an empty place than one that is rented out.

Therefore, you want good tenants who stay for the long term because you'll be able to save money.

They take care of your property: If you establish a solid relationship with your tenants, they will take care of your property and help it to last a long time. If a problem does occur with the rental, they will be more likely to try and fix it themselves rather than letting it become a problem for others in the future. Good tenants tend to be clean, neat, and take care of their rental property for the long term.

You don't have to worry about problems from tenants: If you have a good relationship with your tenant, you're less likely to have trouble with them. If there are problems or maintenance issues, it's far easier to resolve them if you know who your tenant is. It's much harder if the person is an unknown entity that could potentially cause damage or even be a liability in the future (i.e., they have a criminal record).

You can enjoy more free time: If you have good tenants who pay the rent on time, it will take less of your time to manage your rental income. Consequently, you'll be able to spend more of your free time with friends and family and doing other things that you enjoy. This is another big benefit of owning rental properties because if you do it right, you can make money without much effort or without ever having to lift a finger.

They will build strong friendships with you: If you treat tenants well and they feel like they can trust you, they will feel more comfortable and open with you. This will lead to a deeper connection, and that in turn makes it easier to get referrals from your tenant. They will also be more likely to take out references for future tenants.

Therefore, if you manage to attract good tenants, it's going to be very rewarding in the long term because it will give you more opportunities to expand your rental business.

It will help you to understand your tenants better: It's a great advantage to know the people that are renting out your properties. Since they live in the same neighborhood, they have likely dealt with similar problems. Knowing what they have experienced can help you to understand their needs better and make them more comfortable. You'll also be able to learn what works best for managing your properties and creating new opportunities for growth.

You'll have a good reputation: When people see that you've developed a good relationship with your tenants, they are likely to want to rent from you. They'll want to rent from you because they see it as an opportunity to get a fair deal and enjoy the experience of renting from someone who has their best interests in mind. Word spreads quickly, and people will tell others who they know that are looking for a place to rent. Therefore, if you have a good tenant, it will lead to more referrals.

It will give you confidence: If you feel good about the relationship that you have with your tenants, it's going to make it easier to deal with any problems that arise. It will increase your credibility with your tenants and possibly new clients because they will notice that you are fair and treat them nicely. You won't feel stressed and take on too much responsibility or be hyper-vigilant over the details.

How to Build a Strong Relationship with Your Tenants

Keeping your tenants happy and content at their facilities is the best approach to building a relationship with them. Some tips on how to do this are explained below:

Treat your tenants like family: It is important that you are honest and open with them to make sure they feel comfortable in your facility. If you don't tell them what to expect, then they won't know what you want from them. Telling your tenants where to park, informing them about the location of their new facility, or telling them about potential problems that may occur during their stay is a great way for you to establish a good relationship with your tenants. When you treat your tenants like family, they are going to feel like they are in a much safer environment, safer than their own homes. This makes them feel more open and welcome. When you treat your tenants like family, it also will help them feel great about living there, and this means that they will most likely stay longer.

Set proper expectations in advance: In the beginning, you need to set the right expectations for your tenants. If you do not, then you might not be able to blame your tenants for causing any problems. This will not look good on you, and it could give them the wrong impression about your abilities as an owner. Be very clear about what is acceptable and what is not acceptable in your facility.

For example: if you want them to keep their place clean, then tell them about that upfront and make sure they comply with it. If, after you have given them the rules of your facility and they choose not to follow them, then it is okay to tell them they are no longer welcome in your facility. That will show them that you are serious about what you say. When it comes to setting expectations for your tenants, don't be afraid to tell people how you feel about certain things.

Communicate Regularly: By communicating with your tenants regularly, you will be able to make them feel like they are a part of the family and an important part of that. This will make them cherish the relationship that they have with you as their landlord and, at the same time, make all your efforts worth it. When you want your tenants to stay longer, then you will find it necessary to communicate with them often so that they know what is going on. This way, they know when something needs attention or when there is something new for them to know about. They will be more willing to stay longer because of this communication and because of how caring you are with them as their landlord.

Be honest, friendly, and kind towards your tenants: When you are honest, friendly, and kind to your tenants, they feel completely comfortable in your facility. They also know that you are going to be like their friend as long as they "play nice" with you. When you understand the way people think, it will allow you to use their natural instincts to make them feel comfortable and comfortable in their new home. This makes them feel like they are in a safe environment, and it prevents them from doing anything that would make you upset. They would rather stay in your facility than risk losing it.

Solicit Your Tenants' Input on New Rules: New rules are things that you need to take into consideration when adding them to your facility. For example: if your tenants tell you they want a swimming pool, then go ahead and add one, but you need to keep in mind that this added expense will mean less income for you. When adding new rules and regulations, discuss with your tenants to make sure they are all on board with what you have planned. When you take the time to discuss things with your tenants, it shows them that you care about their opinions, and it makes them feel welcome.

Respect their relationship with the property: While you might be the landlord and in charge of making the rules, don't forget that tenants have their own relationship with the property. They have their own opinions about how it should be managed and how it should be kept. If you are not careful, you could end up hurting your tenants' feelings or causing conflict between them and yourself. When your tenants love where they live, they will stay there longer, and they will tell their friends about how great the facility is. Staying loyal will mean that you have fewer expenses as a landlord since you won't have to replace them right away if one of them decides not to renew their lease. If your happy tenant decides to move out, then you have just gained a referral for someone who is willing to rent your place. This will save you time in screening potential tenants and also money on advertising.

Listen: When it comes to establishing a good relationship with your tenants, listening is the most important thing that you can do. As a landlord, you need to listen to what they want and make sure they are completely happy with where they live. When you listen to your tenants, they will feel like they are important to you. That will make them want to stay longer in your facility because they know that it is important to you that they stay. Listening is also a great way for your tenants to tell you what their concerns are and how happy or unhappy they are with their surroundings. If you listen to your tenants, then they will respect you more because you are showing them courtesy and respect by listening.

Make them a part of the community: If you want your tenants to feel like they belong, then you need to make them feel like they are a part of the community. You can do this by having social gatherings at the facility or hosting an event that is fun and enjoyable. In order for your tenants to feel like they belong in your facility, then you need to make sure they feel an attraction to it. This will help them remain there longer and may even encourage them to invest in it as well. Getting people together will also bring out the good side of others so that everyone can truly enjoy themselves. This atmosphere will be inviting for everyone, so don't tell anyone that this is just for your tenants, or it won't work effectively.

Make your facility look good: The first impression is the last impression. This means that a building or property will be considered great and wonderful when it looks good. Make sure that it is clean, attractive, and well- maintained to attract the interest of potential tenants for long-term rental of your facility. In order for a place to look good and presentable, you need to take care of it regularly. Keeping the facility clean will keep people from feeling unsafe in it, which will attract them more towards it. The tenant-landlord relationship in a well-maintained building will obviously be great too.

Ensure that the facility is well managed: If you have a good manager, then they would take care of all things that have to do with managing your facility, from upkeep to repairs and maintenance. This will make people feel comfortable so that they don't want to leave the place after staying for a short period of time. If you want your tenants to stay longer, then you need to ensure that your place is well managed. When the management is keen on establishing relationships with tenants, then they will keep their eyes on the ball when it comes time for them to be responsible for keeping everything in order. This will make them more focused on the positive aspects of their facility and not all the negative things.

Show them how you care: Make it a point to tell your tenants that you care about them whenever you have the chance to do so. If there is something at your facility that is bothering them, tell them about this and get their feedback about what they think should be done to make the place better. This will let you understand what they want and how it can be achieved by giving them more control over what needs attention. In doing so, you can motivate the tenants to make changes that will encourage your efforts in making the place great for all of your tenants.

Allow them to add their own touches: If you want to have a good relationship with your tenants and want them to stay longer, then you need to give them the chance to add their personal touches as well. When they have the chance to do so, they will be more willing to stay longer and make improvements on what needs attention. This will also make them feel like they are a part of the family and not just some random stranger that is renting your facility. In giving them this opportunity, you are also giving yourself a chance at making the property a better asset for all of your tenants, who will most likely look for other places because of what a great place this is.

Provide free maintenance: When you want to have a good relationship with your tenants, then you need to provide them with the opportunity to have their property maintained by a qualified professional. This will make them feel like they are being taken care of and that you care about the things that concern them. They will be sure to stay longer for this reason and because they feel like they are being taken care of.

Provide plenty of incentives: You can also use different incentives that are beneficial for both your tenants and yourself as an owner to get them to appreciate your facility even more. These incentives can be anything like giving discounts on the rent, giving them more personal space, or even providing great amenities that they can have access to. By choosing one of these ideas as an owner, you will be able to get your tenants to appreciate your facility even more and make them stay longer than they would normally do. As an owner, you will find that it is worth it to have loyal tenants because they are sure to care about their surroundings much better than just some random person who is renting the property for a short period of time.

Make a move smoother: Another way to build a good relationship with your tenants and make them feel more comfortable is to make their move smoother by providing them with professional movers for an affordable price. With these professionals, the movers will be able to load, unload and transport their property from theircurrent place to your rental without causing any damage. They are also capable of setting up all of the tenant's furniture so that it goes smoothly, in addition to buying any new furniture for them if necessary.

Reduce monthly costs: One of the ways that you can build a great relationship with your tenants and entice them to stick around for longer periods is by making sure that they have affordable monthly rent and by keeping their expenses low as well. By doing this, you can let them know that they are not being taken advantage of and, at the same time, keep up with your expenses on maintenance and repairs while keeping it affordable for all your tenants.

Ways in Which Landlords Lose Good Tenants

Having a good tenant is something that every landlord strives for. However, sometimes you get unlucky, and your good tenant moves out. This is bad because it takes time to find a new tenant, and they may or may not want to move into your property. So, it's important the landlord does whatever they can to keep their existing tenants happy in order to avoid having to find new tenants. The following are ways in which landlords lose good tenants:

Failing to fix major issues: The most common issue that ruins a landlord-tenant relationship is when the landlord is unwilling to repair something. If you have mold, then you need to make sure it is removed. If you have a hole in your roof, then you need to fix it or purchase a new one. If there are leaks in the house, then you need to fix that as well before the problem grows and becomes an even larger problem. It's possible to negotiate with your tenant; however, if the problem is with the house itself, then you should inform them that you can't fix it because it is caused by something that is beyond your control. If they want out of the lease, then so be it.

It's better to lose a good tenant than to let them live in a bad house.

Not Supporting New Tenants: If you have a lot of properties and don't have time to manage them properly, it's best if you get a manager who can take care of new tenants. You might lose a good tenant if you don't do this, and they decide to leave because they are unable to live in the property properly or all their needs are not being met. You should also support your new tenants by providing them with information about the house, neighborhood, and anything else that will help them to live in your property and be good tenants. This can help you to avoid future issues and having unhappy tenants.

Repeatedly raising rent: This is one of the worst things that a landlord can do, and it's the biggest reason why good tenants leave. Raising rent is something that you want to avoid if possible, and it's best not to do it unless needed. However, you will need to raise your rent to keep up with escalating living costs in some instances. If you are raising rent, then try to give a good amount of notice first so that they can prepare properly. Make sure you are only increasing rent by a reasonable amount, usually no more than 5%. It can be a bad idea to increase rent more often than once per year when you don't need to.

Failing to respect tenant privacy: A lot of landlords make the mistake of invading their tenants' privacy. The worst thing you can do is to spy on someone without their permission. This can cause a lot of issues and lead to bad situations between landlord and tenant. If you're going to spy on one of your tenants, then make sure it's for a legitimate reason, like when they are doing something wrong with the house or being dishonest with you. It's best not to spy on them at all and do it legally. It is not a good idea to spy on a tenant without their consent. Not only will this cause issues, but it's also illegal, and you could be sued for it.

Not Communicating: Communication is the key to dealing with your tenants and making sure that you don't lose them to other landlords. In order to keep your tenants happy, it's essential to be able to answer their questions, respond when they need you, and most importantly create a written record of all the things that are going on in your property. This will help you manage your property better and can also be used when you need it as a reference later on. It will also help prevent problems from occurring before they happen because it gives everyone involved an idea of what is going on in the house and how things will be handled in case of an emergency or if there's an issue that needs to be solved.

Failing to conduct tenants screening properly: If you are a landlord, then you need to check the tenants that are renting the property and make sure that they meet all your requirements before they move in. To do this right, then it's important that you conduct a thorough screening process for them both before and after they move in to ensure that there are no issues with the property. This will stop a lot of issues from occurring and will also prevent your property from being damaged or broken down by one of your tenants.

Allowing the property to deteriorate: You must make sure that your property is in good condition. If you are not taking care of it, it will lose the charm and attractiveness that tenants will look for when they move in. It's up to you to make sure that everything works properly and that the repairs have been done properly so that your tenants will feel comfortable living there.

Being unprofessional: Being unprofessional can cause a lot of problems for both you and your tenants. If you're an unprofessional landlord, then your property may be viewed as lower quality, and this could mean that people don't rent it, or they move away quickly. They may end up feeling like they have to do everything while they are renting the property, which makes them work harder than they normally would when living in their own home. It's important that you are always on top of your game and keep a professional image because if not, then you could run into some issues with problems in the house or with your tenants being unhappy with the way you're managing things.

Not Preparing the House for New Tenants: Sometimes, when a tenant moves out, you may realize that you didn't do some maintenance. This is something that you need to prepare for and include in your budget if possible. If you don't prepare the property properly, then there's a chance that your new tenants won't like it and will find somewhere else to live. By preparing the house, you can make it look nicer, more appealing, and potentially increase your chances of finding new tenants. It's best if you spend some time cleaning up the property too so that they will be able to move in without having to worry about cleaning it themselves right away.

Not Investing in Upgrades: Upgrading the property is something that is important for any landlord, especially if you have a nice property. If you don't upgrade your property, then it's possible for them to fall behind in quality and make them look worse than competing properties nearby. This is why it's best to budget for regular upgrades so that you can maintain your property at a high standard. This can help you decrease your vacancy rate and increase the chances of keeping good tenants.

This entails adding accessories such as chandeliers to your rental property just to improve its aesthetics.

Not Understanding Tenant Needs: One of the worst things that happen when a tenant moves out is when the new tenant complains about something you didn't know about before and wasn't prepared for. You should always get to know your tenant before you let them move in so that you can understand their needs better. This can help prevent future problems from occurring and allow you to have a good relationship with your tenants.

Not Building Trust: Building trust is one of the most important things to look out for when you're a landlord.

You should always build up a good reputation with all your tenants because it can help to decrease your vacancy rate, which in turn increases the amount of money you make. Usually, when you do anything illegal, such as using their security deposit to pay for something else, it does not help towards building up any trust at all. This can be why so many tenants walk away from their landlords and choose to move in somewhere else where they know that they'll be treated better.

Not Having Good Boundaries: This is an important skill for landlords to have, and it's something that you should work on. There will be times when tenants will have issues with their neighbors or other tenants. It's also important to know when you're allowed to go into someone else's property and repair things so that you don't bug your tenants and cause problems for them. If you have good boundaries, then it means that you'll have fewer complaints from your tenants about what goes on in the neighborhood or the property.

Not Keeping Up With Their Bills: Being a landlord is hard work, and it can be a lot of work to keep up with the tasks that are necessary in order to run the property and make sure that everything is in good working order. This is hard to do at times, but you should always try your best because it's better for them if they have a place to live that they feel good about and is something that they want. If you don't keep up with their bills, then you may face problems with late payments and, in turn, get a bad reputation which could be damaging for your business in the long run.

Not Giving Tenants Enough Freedom: Failing to give tenants enough freedom with renting a property is something that can greatly affect your business. You should moderate the amount of freedom you give your tenants on your property. If you give them all the freedom they need, then it's possible that they will start to get things wrong and not fix them when they break. This could also be harmful to your operations as a landlord and can cause problems for other tenants on the property, and it could potentially damage relationships if there are others living there too. Sometimes, it's best to talk to them about this first and have an agreement between you on what they can do and to ask permission before getting work done on the house or making changes.

Not Providing a Good Location: This is one of the key factors that can affect your rental property because it will determine how well you can rent out your property and whether or not you'll be able to get good tenants for it. If you have a good location, then there are more people who will be interested in renting from you, and this can cause severe competition over the property. This is why it's important to be located in a good place that is easy to access but also secure so that there are fewer problems when the tenants are living there. A property may be good, but the location may make good potential tenants reconsider renting there.

What Do Good Tenants Want?

The following are some of the things tenants look for when renting out property:

Security: Renters should be concerned with security, especially in today's world where things aren't what they used to be. Renters are looking for a location where they feel safe and secure. This means that the neighborhood is well-lit, with visible police patrols. The security office should have a 24-hour security guard to monitor the premises. The building should be gated, with individual units monitored by video surveillance. Not only will it keep troublemakers away from your property but also it will also offer you peace of mind as a landlord. Without security, no one is going to feel comfortable renting a property. It's the landlord's responsibility to make sure that there is security so that anyone who lives on the property is safe.

Local Amenities: This is another thing tenants look out for when moving into a new home. They would like to know what kind of amenities are available for them so they can choose if they want to stay or move on if these amenities are not accessible to them. This is very important because tenants would rather not spend money on activities that they won't get to enjoy, let alone travel back and forth from a rental property. To make this easier for tenants, they should find out if there's a community center near their new home, which will allow them to participate more in the activities. They want to know if there's a pool, gym, or playground nearby. A printer, a business center, and a convenience store are also considered amenities that tenants look for in their rental homes or units. When a tenant feels that their needs are already met, they will be more inclined to commit to their new home.

Proximity to other Homes and Schools: Another big concern of renters is whether they are going to be close enough to their neighbors. No one would like to live in a neighborhood where they have to be concerned with what their neighbors are doing. If the tenants in your location will be close enough to know their neighbors, then you may want to consider that as a plus. At the same time, you may want to consider where the nearest schools are for young families. Also, think about the proximity of other homes and other businesses, as well.

A homey feeling: Most renters want to live in a homey feeling environment. They are looking for a safe and secure home where they can feel at home and where their neighbors will be friendly towards them. A nice, nook-like space with lots of natural light is perfect for a person who wants to feel as though they are living in a very relaxed atmosphere.

Easy Access to Public Transport: Public transport is one of the main ways that renters can get to and from home. If the property is located along with some type of public transport, the renters will be very pleased with the location. Many renters choose to rent an apartment or a house in order to save on gas and other transportation expenses. By being close to public transit, they will not have to worry about these extra expenses.

Distance to Work: Most people choose a rental property that is located within close proximity to their work. This will save them more time, as they won't have to spend too much time commuting and they'll have enough energy to finish their work without the hassle of traffic. Tenants should also take note of the upcoming shopping areas or business centers that might affect their living environment. Either way, it's best if a rental property is near their workplace or schools for easy access and convenience.

Cleanliness and Neatness: A rental property should be well-maintained, clean, and pristine. The pretty appearance should be maintained, as well. This means that the property should have a professional cleaning service on a regular schedule to keep the home spotless at all times. The house should also be orderly. It should not look like there is any trash lying around or food on the floor or in the sink.

Furnishings: Renters check out the floor plan of a residential property if it has furnished rooms or not. If you own a furnished property, try to match the furniture of your other units to have a uniform look for your location.

For example, you can put in modern furniture for your units if you are planning on renting properties that are new. If you have older properties that have been renovated, then you can still install modern décor.

Good Neighbors and Good Neighborly Relationships: Renters want to know that their neighbors are friendly and polite. At the very least, they should not be loud or disruptive.

They will want to feel as though their neighbors have a good relationship with each other and that they are safe from danger due to the fact that there is a high police presence in the area. If the residents do not get along, then many tenants will not like this location and will tend to avoid it at all costs.

Access to a Green Environment: Finally, renters are very interested in living in a green neighborhood. If the area has a lot of green space, the tenants will feel as though they are staying in the "city that never sleeps." They will also feel as though they are staying near shopping and dining centers, which gives them more options with regard to food and other services. With a location close to these centers, people will be able to get their exercise as well.

Closest Shopping Center: When buying a property, most renters want to be near their favorite shopping malls or commercial centers. These places offer them lots of things to do, and they can get away from the stress at work. If your residential properties are close to these places, then it's more likely that tenants will consider moving in. If their kids go to schools nearby and their children will be able to attend good schools, then they'll feel more confident about renting your property. When tenants are in a new city for the first time and struggling to adjust, shopping malls are also a great place for them to vent out their anger and frustration with other people's harsh comments.

Maintenance and Repairs Costs: When tenants move into a property, they take note that if it is well- maintained, they will save money on repairs and maintenance costs. An unkempt property can get expensive to fix up, so renters will be more likely to keep the unit clean if it's well-maintained. When tenants look at their options in a new neighborhood or city, they'll be more relaxed knowing that their rental property is not like a slum. They are also more willing to commit if people in their community are willing to keep the property clean and well-maintained.

History of the Area: People tend to judge a home by its past. So, renters would like to go for properties that have a good reputation. They don't want to move into some run-down apartment or even a new building where there's no history of the area. This gives them an idea of how people treat other people and how they operate their property. They would also be more likely to commit if they are comfortable with their surroundings.

Availability of Utilities: Tenants should check out rental properties that are able to provide utilities such as water, electricity, and gas. This is important because tenants can't afford to waste their money on bills that they don't need to pay. If the property is able to provide them with utilities, then they'll know that they won't spend a lot of money on bills and that they will be able to save more.

Chapter 4:

Handling Leases and Pricing

A lease is a commitment between a landlord and a tenant to give the property for a specific period of time to the tenant unless either party gives the notice to terminate the agreement. You should remember that not all leases are created equal, and some can be very unfavorable for tenants depending on their individual circumstances prior to signing this document. The lease agreement sets the guidelines for both the landlord and tenant to follow and violating this agreement may result in serious legal consequences. This chapter will mainly focus on the basics of leases and determining the rent prices for your property.

The Basics of Writing a Lease

A lease should clearly state the terms and conditions of renting a property. The following are the steps to follow when writing a lease agreement:

Title and Format Your Document: The lease should include the title, date of execution, and the legal name of the landlord (if different from the owner). The title of the lease can be as simple as "Lease Agreement" and should be centered and bolded. The document should be typed, signed, and dated in red ink.

Make a list of lease provisions: It's important to provide a list of all the provisions that will be included in the lease. The lease should provide for how long the tenant will be leasing the property and include the renewal terms. You can also include parking rights, tenants' utility payment responsibilities, and other terms that you deem fit.

Add detail to all the provisions listed: Provide detail to every provision listed in the lease. For example, if the lease states that "tenants should not host parties at the property," then you need to define any terms associated with hosting a party. Some of the important provisions include:

Leased Property

You should give a thorough description of the property to be leased in your lease agreement, such as the size of each room, appliances and furnishings, space for parking, and any infrastructure problems such as mold or mildew. You should also list any improvements that have been made to the property or will be made in the future. The description of the premises must also include conditions that apply to all tenants, as well as how you will determine if they are satisfactory.

Rent and Rent Increase

It is important that the lease agreement clearly states how much rent will be paid, how often it will be paid, and whether or not you can increase the rent once the lease begins. It is also important that you include a clause stating when this can occur in your agreement. You should also include a clause stating that if you decide to increase the rent, then you must first give the tenant an unreasonable notice for breach of any term of the lease and then give them thirty days advance notice of your intent to raise the rent. You can also include a provision stating that increases for major capital improvements must first be approved by the local authorities in writing before they are made.

Late Fees

It is important to include a clause stating that if any payment of rent is late, then it will be considered a breach of the lease agreement. You should also include a clause stating that if rent is unpaid or paid late on three separate occasions, then the tenant will be considered to be in default and will have three business days to cure their default, or they must vacate the unit. You should also state whether or not the tenant will be allowed to make up any late fees in the future.

Responsibilities for Maintenance and Repair Services

You should outline the responsibilities of both tenant and landlord for maintaining the premises in a satisfactory condition to prevent serious problems from occurring.

You should also include a clause stating that it is the responsibility of both parties to pay for any repairs or maintenance services and the obligation to ensure that all utilities such as electricity, water, and sewerage are working properly.

Tenant's Insurance

You should include a clause in the lease agreement stating that all tenants must have coverage for their belongings and property against damage or loss as a result of fire and theft. The policy must also specifically mention whether or not it will reimburse the tenant for any damages to another party's property or items left inside the unit. You should also include a provision that states any costs incurred for the repair and replacement of damaged property of the tenant will be deducted from the security deposit.

Deposit

It is important that you include a clause in your lease agreement stating that the tenant must pay a security deposit of at least ten percent of the total rent. The landlord must also provide evidence that they have kept a record of all monies collected. The security deposit should be held in a separate account until the tenant vacates the premises and is sent to the landlord, at which time it will be returned to them with an accounting clearly outlining any deductions made from it by either party.

Occupancy

The lease agreement should only be considered fully completed when the tenant has moved into their unit. If a tenant vacates the premises, then the lease agreement should include a provision stating that the tenant will be responsible for all rent owed for any period of time remaining on your lease agreement. If you are giving the notice to move out and your tenant does not exit the property within 60 days, then they will also have to pay you for such an unused period of time.

Notice of Default

To terminate a lease early, both parties should agree on a common procedure that will be followed when either party has defaulted on the agreement. It is also necessary for you to have the authority to evict a tenant from your unit even if they are not breaching any terms of the lease if you feel that they have violated any provisions. You should include a clause in your lease agreement stating that thirty days' written notice must be sent by either party to terminate the lease by law. If such notice is not given, then an eviction proceeding may be brought against them in court.

Eviction Notice

To evict a tenant from your property, you should include a clause in your lease agreement stating that the eviction notice will be served by either posting or delivering it personally to the tenant. You should also state whether or not an additional form of service such as email will be considered valid when serving notices on tenants as they may not be entitled to receive mail at an address.

Write in a list of tenant obligations

The obligation set forth by both parties is what defines a lease agreement. The tenant should be obligated to pay for all rent and the lease term, and the landlord is obligated to provide certain amenities such as maintenance and repair services. The landlord should also provide for any utilities that may be required by the tenant. It's important to specify in this agreement what policies are in place for tenants to follow in regard to rules regarding pets, parties, and security.

Public Health and Safety

It is important that your lease agreement provides a clause that states you are in charge of providing a safe environment for your tenants and guests to stay on the premises. This provision should provide you with a right to enter your unit at any time necessary for inspection as well as when there is a health and safety problem, but only if you notify the tenant by calling them on the phone or sending them written notice within 24 hours of such an event. The notice must be provided in writing so that it can be proven at court hearings in the event of a dispute.

Check Local Laws: When writing a lease, it's important to check local laws since this document can affect the financial and legal stability of both the landlord and his tenant. For example, some US states do not allow landlords to raise the rents beyond a certain amount.

These rent increases should be spelled out in the lease. In other states, landlords can increase rent prices to cover normal wear and tear on the property, such as fixing broken windows or replacing carpets.

Create a Signature Section: A lease should have a section that allows both parties to sign the agreement. To make this process more secure, you can include a specific date to execute this procedure. Signatures make the lease agreement legally binding.

There are additional components you can add to the lease which may improve it. They are as follows:

Appliances included in the rental: When coming up with a lease agreement with your tenants, it is important to list and describe additional appliances that are provided in your rental unit for the tenant's use. You can include additional information regarding the appliances such as cookers, refrigerators, dishwashers, and microwaves. It is also important to include a statement indicating the condition they are in when the client is moving in. It is important that you include a clause in the lease agreement stating that if your tenant has damaged any of your appliances and then fails to pay for the repair, then you can deduct the cost from your tenant's security deposit or rent. You should also include a clause stating that any repairs outside of normal wear and tear can be deducted from your tenant's security deposit or rent. You can also deduct the cost of repairs after one month if it arises during their tenancy.

Abandonment: If you suspect that your tenant may intend to abandon the unit, then it is important to include a statement in the lease agreement that allows you to take back the property still in possession of the tenant. You can include a clause in your rental unit saying that if the tenant abandons or gives up possession of your rental unit, then you or any member affiliated with you may retake possession and demand immediate payment for rent owed by your tenant.

Bad neighbor clause: A bad neighbor clause is a clause in a lease agreement that allows your tenant to terminate their lease agreement if problems with another neighbor arise. The clause should be in writing, state the name of the tenant, and refer to the neighbor by their name. The agreement should also ask your tenant to notify you of any problems with a neighbor if they arise.

Breaches and Disputes: It is common for conflicts to arise between landlords and tenants regarding breaches that can arise during the course of your tenancy. If you suspect that this may happen, you should include a clause in your lease agreement stating that disputes between you and your tenant will be resolved by arbitration or mediation. The clauses should also list some examples of disputes that are likely to occur, such as noise disturbances during 6 PM on Mondays through Fridays or during peak hours from 8 AM until 8 PM on weekdays.

Lease Termination Provision for Military Personnel: The Landlord-Tenant Act allows a tenant to terminate the lease agreement early if they are a member of the armed forces who has been deployed for at least 180 days. The tenant is also required to have written permission from their commanding officer and then give you thirty days' notice. The tenant is required to pay rent until the tenancy ends in accordance with your original lease agreement.

Pet Fees: If your tenant has pets in their rental unit, then it is important to include a clause in the lease agreement that allows the landlord to charge a fee for their care during their tenancy. This clause can be used to ensure that tenants do not keep pets on the premises that may infringe on their health and safety. Note: This should be included at the end of the lease agreement so as not to violate any of the tenant's rights under State or Federal law.

Subletting: A lease agreement should include a provision stating whether or not your tenant can sublet their unit; if they do, then they must notify you in writing at least thirty days before they begin subletting. The tenant is also to give you written notice of any responsibility they may have to pay you for utilities, rent, or profits when subletting.

Utilities: It is important that agreements include a clause stating whether or not the tenant will be responsible for paying their own utilities such as electricity, water, and sewerage. You can do this by stating, "If you neglect to pay your utility bills at least one month late, then we can remove your utilities until the bill is paid." It is also important to include various clauses within the lease agreement, such as whether or not the rent will increase if there are problems with electrical or water distribution lines.

Keys, gates, and Garages: It is important that you include a clause in the lease agreement stating whether or not your tenant will have their own keys to the premises and give you written notice if they decide to move out early. Consider including a clause stating that your tenant must leave the gate in a satisfactory condition and state whether or not you will reimburse them for any costs incurred due to damage done by their pets. You should also include a clause that states whether or not your tenant will be able to use the garage for storage. The clause should state whether or not it will be available for the tenant's exclusive use. Additionally, it should detail any conditions that may apply, such as how you will determine if the space is satisfactory.

Extended Absence by Tenant: If your tenant is going to be absent from the state for an extended period of time, then it is important to include a clause in the lease agreement stating that you will have access to the property for inspections and maintenance. This should also include a clause that gives you the right to enter your premises at any time after a notice of intent to enter was given and at least 24 hours before you enter.

Inspection Conditions: It is important that you include a clause in the lease agreement allowing you access to your rental unit according to inspection conditions set forth by law or industry standards. You also need to state what rights you have after conducting an inspection as well as how often they may occur. The clause should state that you are only allowed to make inspections at a reasonable time and only after you have given the tenant twenty-four hours' notice and made attempts to let them know. You are also required to be present during the inspection, which must be conducted by a certified inspector if requested by the tenant.

Tips for an Awesome Lease

For a lease to be detailed and clear, both parties entering the agreement must make sure that they pay attention to the following points:

Fix Issues Immediately: If the tenant is making poor decisions, you should take action immediately after becoming aware of these. For example, if the tenant does not pay his rent on time and you find out that he has moved out, you should immediately make another visit to the property and collect unpaid rent. If the tenant ends up moving into a subletter's house, you are going to want to pursue legal action in your jurisdiction either by filing a lawsuit or simply seizing his property.

Write everything in detail: At the very beginning of the process, you need to write down all the things that are wrong with the property and include them in your lease. If the carpet is stained and you have never noticed it previously, you should mention them in your lease. This helps make sure that both parties clarify everything before a new tenant decides to move in.

Lease Eviction Clause: You should also have an eviction clause in your lease. It is important if you plan on renting out a unit to a long-term tenant because you cannot kick out that person without going through the courts. If the tenant gets in trouble with the police and he is using your rental property, you should be able to evict them without much hassle. You should also keep the statement of this clause in bold letters so as to make sure that it catches the attention of the tenants.

Research the Laws: Before you begin the process of finding tenants, you should make sure that you are operating in accordance with the laws. This means that when you accept tenants, you will not face any legal hurdles or potential legal problems. For example, if a tenant has been using illegal drugs on your property, he is going to be arrested and sent to jail. You may not have to face a lawsuit, but the tenant may still file a case against you in court.

Tailor your lease: You should tailor your lease to the needs of your tenants. Many examples may be found on the internet, but you should always add a few clauses to make it more flexible for your needs. For example, you may want to make sure that the tenant is not allowed to have any pets in his house.

For this case, you can simply add such a clause in your lease and also specify what will happen if that rule is broken.

Use proper language in your lease agreement: You should include all the important details in your lease agreement and make sure that your tenant understands everything. For example, if you do not allow pets, you can specify the type of dog that is allowed or even the breed. Using proper language will make sure that no misunderstandings or extra fees arise from your tenants.

Avoid Strict Provisions: It's important that both parties are responsible for their actions and responsibilities. For example, if the tenant rents out the premises to a subletter, he should be liable for any damages caused by this person. If the landlord has a strict rule against pets and then allows his tenant to get one, he should be responsible for any damages caused by this pet.

Decide on Termination: A lease should clearly state how the termination of the lease can take place. For example, you can decide that the tenant will be given a certain amount of notice if he is going to terminate his lease. You may also decide that if he has not paid rent by a certain date, the lease will automatically terminate.

Arrange Maintenance and Repairs: Among the most important parts of a lease is what happens when there are maintenance and repair issues. If the tenant breaks an appliance, it's important to state how much compensation the landlord will pay for this. You may also want to ask both parties who pay for repairs if someone isn't paying for these expenses.

Follow the Law: The law may change, which means it's important to update the lease agreement as needed. If you have a strict rule on pets and then allow this, you should include a new rule in your lease agreement. You should also follow the laws regarding how much notice you must give before you can start eviction proceedings.

Challenges Faced When Making a Lease Agreement

The following are some of the challenges faced when making a lease agreement:

Finding the right tenant: Finding the right tenant to get into a lease agreement with is a major challenge. The landlord should make sure that he's creating a lease agreement with someone who has a good credit history, previous history of paying rent on time and is stable. An inexperienced landlord is often not able to find such a reliable tenant. The landlord needs to inspect each of his prospective tenants' backgrounds and see if he would accept moving into the chosen home. This is quite time- consuming and involves the risk that a good tenant will drop out, and the landlord may not be able to find another one as fast as he had hoped.

Writing the Lease Agreement: The landlord needs to be very careful when he writes the lease agreement, especially when it is for a new tenant. It's hard for a landlord to convey his exact thoughts on how the lease agreement should be written. Therefore, a landlord should draft the lease agreement before he tries to get his tenant to sign it. If there are any errors in the agreement, it could cause problems later on.

Get Tenant to Sign lease Agreement: To make the lease agreement valid, the landlord must get the signatures of the tenant on paper. There is a lot of pressure because if he can't get his tenant to sign, he will have to find another tenant and start all over again. This could lead to them making mistakes in the process, and it's very likely that he'll lose a decent tenant he was able to find.

Making changes to a lease agreement: When a landlord makes changes to a lease agreement, it is a very complicated process. First, the landlord must have the authority to make changes to a lease agreement. If he does not, he will be sued for falsifying documents. Then he must make sure that each change is drafted in the correct language and make sure all the necessary signatures are present.

Avoiding a Dispute in the Event of an Eviction: At times, disputes may arise during the eviction of tenants.

Once you file for eviction, it can be very difficult to undo this process. The landlord should basically sit back and wait for the tenant to move out without making any additional steps toward this end. He should never use force, scare tactics or try to get the tenant to leave.

Determining the rate to charge for rent

Before you start placing the rental unit on the market, you should decide how much you want to charge for it. By doing this, you will be able to determine how much it costs to maintain the property and what your rent amount is when renting out units. Consider these factors:

Your running expenses: It's important to consider your running expenses. These expenses include things such as the cost of utilities, maintenance, taxes, and insurance. It's important that you consider these factors in determining your rent amount. Competition is always present when there is a large number of rental units available. For example, if you are in suburbia and are offering a one-bedroom apartment to rent for $900 and there is another person who offers the same unit at the same location at $800, then the person who has lower rental costs may have an advantage in attracting tenants because they will be able to offer lower rents than you.

The only way that you can keep up with this competition if you want your rental unit to be successful is by making sure that your running expenses are kept low. This means that you need to pay close attention to how often your property needs maintenance work done on it.

Land size such as balconies, gardens, and parking: If you have a property with lots of land (a house or townhouse), then you can charge more for it because the land will add to the facilities your tenant will enjoy.

However, if you are looking at an apartment that has a balcony and a garden as well as a parking space, then you can charge more than someone who is looking at an apartment that only offers one or two of these features.

The location of the property: This will also affect your rate to charge for the rental unit. For example, if you are looking at a complex in the downtown area, you may want to charge more for the unit than for a similar unit in suburbia. Keep in mind that the surrounding community can affect your rental unit's value. For instance, if you are renting out a two-bedroom apartment above an art gallery and it is located next to a defunct dumpster fire on Collins St., then there is some risk of fire or explosion with this location, so don't assume that it's an acceptable one simply because it is close to good local shops and restaurants.

Seasonality: Demands for your rental units will vary throughout the year, which will determine the rental rate at a given time. If you are running a vacation home, for example, it's important to consider how high the demand for this property is during peak seasons such as summer and winter. Rental properties in this country are seasonal, and there are many households that rely on rental assistance payments throughout the year. Therefore, it makes sense to rent out a one-bedroom apartment from around the beginning of May through the end of October because it will be more likely to attract tenants during these months. However, if you are willing to rent out your unit at any time, then you can do so and will still be able to get a good return on investment.

Competitiveness: When determining your rental rate, be aware of how competitive your rental unit is compared to others in the area. For example, if there are many similar properties in the area and each of these rents $2,000 per month, your demand may be reduced. However, if you offer something unique that is not offered by other properties nearby, it can increase your demand and rental rate.

Age and quality of your Property: Consider how expensive your property is compared to others in the area. If your rental unit is older and may need repairs more often than newer ones, this will drive down the demand for your rental property. However, if you have a brand- new unit that stands out among others in the area, this can raise the demand for your rental property.

Consider what other landlords are charging: When determining your rent amount, it is important to consider the rent charged by other landlords for similar properties in the area. If the average rent for a vacation home is $2,000 per month, you may want to charge as much or a little more than this.

The shape and size of the rental unit: If you are getting a full-sized unit with an attached garage, then you will likely want to charge more for it. This is because you will be responsible for repainting, fixing minor damages, and making minor repairs. If the unit is a studio or 1 bedroom apartment that has no attached garage or storage room and only some landings or stairs, then you can charge less. You should also consider the situation of 'The Battle of the Balconies.' In this case, if there are two balconies in one unit and the one on top is bigger than the one on the bottom, then it should be considered as a higher floor area and therefore worth more than the units below it. You can estimate the cost of maintaining a rental unit by calculating how much it would cost to maintain a similar unit somewhere else. For instance, if you are charging $400 for a studio unit and you want to charge $600 for a one-bedroom apartment, then you should investigate how much it costs to maintain the same one- bedroom apartment.

Research on local prices for rentals in a given area: Research on local rental prices for similar properties in the area will help you determine what your price should be. It can help you decide on how much you can charge for the rental units, though it's not a perfect indicator.

Consider the value of your amenities: When renting vacation homes, especially luxury ones, you may want to consider how much your amenities are worth. This may include things such as the number of bedrooms and bathrooms and other unique amenities that you have.

Some properties have beautiful views of lakes or can be rented for parties and special occasions, for example. For example, if you are looking at a studio apartment for rent near the beach with a 5-block walk to the water, then you can charge more for it than someone who is looking at apartments at the same building but has to drive 10-15 minutes to get to the beach. A walkway that is lit up and has lots of people passing by will also give your tenant a sense of security and, therefore, may be worth more than a unit that has an unlit footpath.

Consider the traffic in a given area: If the location of your rental property is too remote from major roads or points of interest, this could reduce the demand for your rental property. The issue with this is that it may require you to pay for special transportation for your tenants if they do not have their own cars, which can increase the cost of renting your property.

Beware of Current events: It's important to be aware of any current events that may affect the demand for your property. For example, if there have been numerous cases of persons renting vacation houses being victims of crimes such as murder. Although crime rates have decreased in recent years, it's still important to be aware of this.

Laws that govern the rate to charge for rent: Most states have laws that govern the maximum amount of rent you can charge for a rented property. These laws are in place to stop landlords from charging exorbitant amounts for rent and evicting their tenants. Local laws may also limit the amount of time you can keep a tenant on your property before they are allowed to end the contract with you. If they do not move out, then they become squatters. For example, if you are renting a home in NJ, then it's illegal to charge an annual percentage rate (APR) of more than 12% per year. This means that if you are charging $2,000 per month for the rent, then your monthly rate cannot exceed $266 per month.

Challenges Faced When Pricing Rentals

In a perfect world, rent prices would just go down and stay down. In reality, however, it may not be quite so easy to get what you pay for. When tenants move in, they commit to staying there until the lease is up, and that means all their expenses are on the landlord for the duration of their stay. In addition, the more tenants a landlord can get to move in, the higher their property values and rent prices will be. When setting rental prices, a landlord is most likely to face the challenges explained below:

Low demand for short-term rentals: For short-term rentals, the market is very seasonal. During the peak season for vacationers and business travelers, there will be a lot of competition for properties on the same level as yours. These properties will have high competition that drives down their rent prices more than your own. For long-term rentals, the market is much steadier, and rents are usually not as high; however, it can be difficult to fill vacancies which decrease profits.

High seasonal demand for properties: When properties are in high demand, landlords often have to increase rent prices in order to get new tenants and keep the ones they already have. Vacancies and turnover can be very costly, although many landlords still charge what the market will bear. These properties are perfect for people looking for a quick place to land and pick up and go when the season changes.

High competition: If an area is super popular, competition can be fierce. Competition may drive down the price of properties in the area you are looking to rent, but not always. You can find properties that have been carefully maintained and well taken care of yet still have low competition and high demand for them.

The high crime rate in a given area: If a neighborhood is known for high crime rates or has a reputation, which may affect the price you can charge for your property. Since demand will not be as high in these areas, some landlords may not bother with them and stay away from the area entirely. You may also be forced to charge lower rent rates due to the problem.

Properties in remote areas: If your property is located in a remote area where there is little or no traffic, this can reduce the demand for your property as well. You may need to provide special transportation for tenants or offer lower rates or other incentives to attract them.

High rates of property vacancy: For most landlords, keeping your property filled is crucial to remaining in business. The longer a rental unit stays vacant, the harder it will be to rent and the lower the rent price will become. One solution for this is to increase your advertising budget or find new ways of reaching potential tenants (for example, trying new outlets such as websites and billboards). Another way is to offer incentives such as free gifts or concessions to prospective tenants. This can help them remember your address and encourage them to sign an agreement with you if they are satisfied with what they see.

Low rent prices in a given area: Especially in highly populated areas, this is a big problem for landlords. Landlords in such places can charge lower rates than their competition and still get plenty of tenants. Unfortunately, this lowers the overall rent prices of that city or area as a whole, which can make your property seem less appealing to potential tenants.

Brokers and agents: This may seem like a good opportunity to save on rental costs. However, you should be wary of brokers or agents who are able to get you good rates because they are paying them to you (for example, they receive commissions). Sometimes they will want to push you into signing a contract with their own company, but this can mean that a lot of the profits will go to them instead of you. Be sure to check out their commission rates as well as the qualifications required for their staff before making your decision.

Competition from online short-term rental sites: Nowadays, a lot of people are turning to the Internet for their housing needs. Sites such as Airbnb and VRBO have changed the landscape of vacation rentals by bringing in new investors who can offer properties at lower prices.

The competition from these sites can be tough on landlords, especially if their renters do not stick to the rules set out in the lease agreement. This affects the rental rate in a given area.

Poor property status: If your property is currently illegal or non-conforming, then it may be difficult for you to charge high rates in the area until it is brought up to code. Most landlords who deal with illegal housing will try to tear them down and rebuild them, but this can be quite costly. If your property has recently been illegally converted by your tenant, then they can be held liable for this and may be forced to indemnify you against any legal issues that arise. If you purchase a property that needs major repairs, then you will probably have a difficult time getting it rented at high rates. On the one hand, this could make it tough for you to find good tenants as potential renters are more likely to choose more affordable properties with more up-to-date housing.

The neighborhood: The location of your property is important to consider when trying to attract good tenants. In a prime location, like downtown, you may be able to charge high rates for your house. Your competition and neighbors may not be able to offer the same high rents, too, though. This means that you need to think about whether it is worth it to invest in a prime location.

Chapter 5:

The Money Muncher We Call Vacancy

Many property managers have a difficult time when it comes to vacancy rates, rental expenses, and churn. The landlord understands the importance of cash flow for every commercial property owner, but some properties suffer from vacancies because there is not enough demand. The vacancy can be signs of inactivity or that negotiating with a tenant is difficult.

Causes of Vacancy in Rentals

It is important for a landlord to understand why their rental unit is vacant for a long duration of time if they are facing vacancy problems. Some factors that may lead to a vacancy in rentals are explained in detail below:

High rent: Rent is the most important factor that can cause vacancy in rentals. If the property is located in a high-rent area, then it is inevitable that the landlord will face vacancy problems after a few years of operation. If a property is too expensive, it might encourage a tenant to seek out a similar property for a lower cost. If the owner refuses to reduce rent, it may cause the tenant to vacate and seek more affordable space. Another issue is the constant increment of rent without any good reason. This tends to displease tenants, making them choose to leave.

Poor location of the property: Landlords who are not capable of finding a location that is sought after by tenants are unfamiliar with the local market. This may force them to offer low-rent units. However, it does not work for long because the tenant's choice for similar property will lead to vacancy problems of the rental unit. It's not always easy to find a good location for the property. Some owners spend a lot of time trying to move their vacant properties only to find that their properties are at less desirable locations and cannot be rented.

Broken items: Landlords should not be tempted to neglect their properties. They may neglect the maintenance of their properties and equipment. This can cause significant problems for tenants, who will not want to rent a property that is already broken down. If something in a unit breaks and goes unfixed, it can be upsetting to some tenants and may force them to leave rather quickly.

Bad tenant management practices: Landlords who are not capable of providing quality units are likely to experience vacancies in rentals. Some landlords also engage in dishonest transactions with tenants, such as illegal rent increases or deductions from security deposits. Whenever a tenant is unsatisfied with the services provided by their landlord, they will look for better alternatives. When the services are not satisfactory, such tenants may decide to move away. But if the landlord does not pay enough attention to such problems, it may result in the submission of a complaint to the Consumer Protection Board. Owners that fail to keep an eye on their properties may often be blamed for eviction proceedings by tenants. Another factor that is linked to service is that of the security system and maintenance of the property. If a property has poor maintenance and no security system, it can easily become a target for illegal activities.

Rent not paid on time: A tenant is expected to pay rent on time. If the amount is not paid, the landlord should definitely follow up with the tenant and try to settle an agreement. However, if a tenant starts paying late, it may result in termination by either party. If a tenant is always late for rent payments, then it might be a good idea for the landlord to evict such a tenant as soon as possible before he becomes delinquent in payments. The concept of mandatory deposit may also cause vacancy in rentals due to non-payment of rent or other damages in excess of the deposit amount.

High holding costs: Some landlords have high holding costs, which include leasehold surcharges, legal fees, and strata fees. These holding costs cause problems for tenants as they are unable to pay the required rent while they are in a contract that requires a deposit to be made before rent is paid.

The tenant will not want to keep the rental unit if monthly rental payments are not forthcoming, and it may force them to leave, therefore causing vacancy in rentals.

Troublesome neighbors: Most tenants are looking for a quiet place where they can be undisturbed by their neighbors. If the neighbor is causing problems for the tenants, they will be forced to vacate, which often results in vacancies in rentals. Just like tenants who are not properly managed can cause problems for the landlord, disruptive neighbors can also be a problem for tenants and make them want to move out of their unit.

Landlord's Lack Of Communication: A landlord who cannot communicate well with his tenants will have the most difficulty communicating with them properly and effectively. Oftentimes, a landlord will not have good communication skills. This might be one of the causes that lead to vacancies in rentals. Lack of trust and communication will result in tenants feeling uncomfortable with their surroundings and may even endure problems such as poor maintenance or security.

Eventually, when the tenant is fed up, they might decide to leave.

High Risk Of Crime: If a property is located in a high-crime area, it can result in the loss of the tenant's security. If a landlord rents property to people who have experienced previous illegal activities, it might not be a pleasant experience for them due to fear of being the victim of burglary, hence vacating the property. It is advisable that landlords should only rent their properties to persons who are capable of paying rent on time and also maintain good security for their properties and those of others.

Personal Problems Of Tenant: Personal problems such as divorce, death, or other circumstances may lead to a vacancy in rentals as the person concerned may move out to avoid certain memories or emotions that may be evoked by the rental property. The property's condition, maintenance, and appearance are also important factors to consider in cases of changes within the tenant. If a tenant has a bad experience in their previous unit, it is likely that they will leave and seek another unit for themselves or a family member.

Lack of Amenities: Amenities can be defined as facilities such as cable services, swimming pools, gyms, or internet access. When there is no cable service, a tenant can easily choose another property that offers it. If the swimming pool is not functioning well and its water level is low, this may result in the loss of tenants if they have children who require regular practice for school purposes. Poor maintenance of amenities will also result in vacating of other units. It also depends on what amenities you want your tenants to enjoy in your rental properties. Providing a variety of amenities will most likely make your tenants want to stay longer in your rental unit.

Lack of Space: When a property is not big enough, it is likely that the tenant will decide to seek a better place for themselves and their family. But if a property does not have enough space for children's play, it can be a good idea for landlords to assess their unit before renting it out to tenants. In this case, the landlord will have to pay extra expenses such as hiring an additional nanny or having an extra play area set up in the staircases or other rooms so that children can continue playing in such areas without disturbing the neighbors. A property that has no additional space such as outdoor space or yard can also mean loss of tenants due to the lack of availability of such areas when they are wanted by occupants.

Frequent Repairs And Maintenance Issues: If a property is constantly having repair and maintenance issues, the tenants will become frustrated with their apartment or a rental unit, especially if they do not have other alternative options. The least that landlords can do is to ensure the presence of contractors for any repairs that are being carried out on the property. The presence of contractors will assist in avoiding further issues such as late payment and constant delays in the completion of tasks at hand. If there are always repair issues, the tenant may assume the building is old and may decide to seek out a new place to rent.

Parking Spaces: Parking spaces are very important when it comes to running a rental business and avoiding vacancies. If there are no parking spaces available, tenants will have little choice but to seek out alternative properties that offer additional parking spaces. This is the case, especially for properties close to the city where such parking spaces are in limited supply.

Repairs And Maintenance Of The Property That Requires Surrounding Properties To Be Vacated: Repairs on units that require surrounding units to be vacated could necessitate people living in surrounding units to be evicted even if they have not broken any lease agreement they had signed previously. This causes vacancies in adjacent units. This is if you do not have a good hold on tenants, and you also want to ensure that repairs are carried out in a quick and timely manner. In addition, landlords should discuss their eviction plans with the tenants if they cannot get them out of the property completely, hence avoiding further conflicts between both parties.

When the vacancy rate is high and rental rates are low, personal debt can quickly increase for landlords. If a landlord fails to manage his/her finances well and does not deal with problems in a timely manner, it could lead to an eviction of the owner from their properties in the event they used mortgage financing.

Consequences of having a vacant rental property

Below are some consequences of having a vacant rental property:

The costs of keeping up a vacant unit can be great: If a property is vacant for too long, some tenants may have to turn off the utilities in order to save on costs. The owner might have to install and manage a new electrical system if the previous tenant did not pay for it. Further, the owner may have to call a plumber when pipes freeze if the previous tenant did not pay for them. Other costs such as security and insurance will continue to rack up and make it difficult for an owner to avoid foreclosure on their property since they do not have enough cash flow from rental income from tenants. If an owner does not have to worry about paying for utilities, repairs, and upgrades, they are less likely to take the state of the rental unit seriously. At the first sign of trouble, the owner might decide to ignore it. After all, there is no one living on the property anymore.

The lack of cash flow in the property can be crippling: A vacant house can prevent an owner from having the cash flow to make his mortgage payments. If a landlord fails to make the mortgage payments, he may be forced to abandon the property and deal with foreclosure.

Poor rental rates: If your rental has been vacant for a long time, you may have to reduce the rental fees in order to attract consumers. Sometimes this is successful, but other times it can lead to even more problems for the landlord who is unable to recognize that their current rental rate may be good enough and does not need to lower the rate in order to fill up their properties.

Health risks for the landlord and tenants: If a property remains vacant for a long time, the owner might risk developing mold in their home or office because it was not properly managed. It can cost thousands of dollars to clean up a mold problem and repair any damages caused by the mold. In addition, pests such as rats may enter a home if it is left vacant for too long.

The beauty of the neighborhood could be ruined: If a property is vacant for too long, it can attract attention from neighbors and may become a target for vandalism. It could also affect the neighborhood's property values and make other properties less attractive to potential tenants.

Bad landlord reputation: A landlord who is not managing their property well will have an image problem in the long run even if their tenants are good ones that pay on time and take care of their rental property properly. It may impact their ability to obtain future tenants and can cause a poor financial outcome for the owner as well as a bad reputation from tenants.

Foreclosure suits and bank loss of collateral value: When a property is vacant, the owner will not have any assets in the property, which means they would not be able to pay off the lender if they are sued. The lender will then foreclose on their home and take away all of the owner's equity that is put on their house.

The owner may lose their personal credit rating if they are unable to pay for the rental property: The credit rating is affected if a landlord is not able to make payments on their property with the rent they have collected. The owner may be unable to access credit in the future because of this negative mark against them which can have real-world effects such as not being able to rent an apartment or a car.

A vacant unit is a potential target for vandalism: Some tenants may feel that since the unit is empty, they can break in and then steal anything they want. Since there is no owner to complain to, they might feel that they can get away with the crime. This makes leaving your rental unit vacant as you risk losing appliances in the vacant unit without even knowing it.

A vacant unit attracts squatters and vagrants: These types of people look for opportunities to live without being detected by society. If you leave an empty property, they will most likely assume that there is nobody home and then enter and make themselves at home. Even if there are signs posted on the property saying, "No Trespassing" or "Vacant," it does not stop them from trying to break in anyway.

A vacant property may boost crime rates in the area: As previously mentioned, the vacant property attracts squatters who will bring in all kinds of illegal activity to the house, but it also attracts other people who are engaged in criminal behavior. For instance, burglars looking for new targets might decide to target the unoccupied houses to steal from them and sell the items on the black market. Some people who are involved in illegal activity might decide to use it as a place for their operations because they know that law enforcement does not have any control over it anymore.

A vacant unit may be an attractive nuisance for children: Children love to play in an empty house, but these houses may also have broken windows, holes in the wall, or rotting floorboards that could cause injury or death if not properly attended to. In case of any tragic event, the landlord may be held responsible for failing to ensure the quality of their unit and may be sued by the affected families of the children or even end up facing prison time.

A vacant property is a liability to the owner: The owner of a vacant house is on the hook for protecting the property from vandalism and property theft. The owner of the house has no choice but to install security cameras, keep track of who comes and goes, and get to know people who come to visit his house. This means that the owner will have to maintain detailed records for a period of time greater than that of ordinary renters. This extra chore can lead to errors by not keeping appropriate records or mistakes in billing. Over time, this may jeopardize the owner's ability to maintain insurance coverage on the property.

A vacant property discourages others from moving into an area because they do not like seeing empty houses around them: Some people love the idea of living in a neighborhood full of occupied homes. They will have plenty of people around them to keep them company, and they will also have a better shot at getting to know their neighbors. However, empty houses are not so popular because it makes the neighborhood seem "sketchy" or unsafe. A lot of people do not want to live in an area that is full of vacant units with the knowledge that there is no real property management in place to help them if there is a problem.

How to minimize vacancy in rental property

The following are some of the tips to help minimize vacancy in rentals:

Proper maintenance can reduce vacancy in rental property: Maintenance can have a significant impact on vacancy reduction. If tenants are asked to pay higher utility bills or if they have to deal with issues such as pests, the owner should make sure that these services are being paid for by the tenants in order to avoid higher costs and potential vacancies.

The right tenant mix is important and should be monitored: It is important to have the right tenant mix for a property in order to minimize vacancies. For example, if the landlord has too many tenants that are older or have children and pets, then they will be hard to fill for other tenants. It is best for landlords to go after desirable tenants that are younger and less likely to have the cost of children, pets, or elderly people in their rent.

Advertise on as many free websites as possible: Having a good online presence on websites that people use can really help attract potential tenants. There are many websites that have rental units listed for free for people to see, which helps a landlord get more attention from potential tenants.

Reducing the Rental Rate to Attract Tenants: A landlord should look for ways to advertise their property in order to get more potential tenants. For example, the landlord can lower their rental rate or have it on the property itself to attract potential tenants. It is important for a landlord to have a good online presence, so people see their ad and see that they are still renting the property.

Create a sense of urgency: In order to get tenants to rent the property as soon as possible, an owner should try to create a sense of urgency for potential tenants to move into their property as soon as possible. In some cases, the owner can offer incentives for people like low rent for a month or incentives for signing a lease that is worth about half of the full rental amount.

Be responsive and attentive: In order to attract potential tenants, it is important for a landlord to be responsive and attentive. This can include taking phone calls from potential tenants and being available at a time that is convenient to them.

Build a good relationship with existing tenants: A landlord can build a good relationship with their current tenants, which can help them attract other tenants in the future. They can do so by visiting with their renters on a regular basis and soliciting feedback on what adjustments or upgrades they would like to see in the property.

Coordinate moving dates well in advance: When a tenant plans on relocating, it is important for a landlord to schedule the move well in advance so that they remember and are able to move their tenants in as soon as possible. They can do this by coordinating the dates of the lease, moving, and paying the rent with their tenant.

Having a good lease agreement: A landlord can help reduce vacancy by having a good lease agreement for their tenants. It is important for the tenant to sign the lease agreement and understand it if they are moving in. If the tenant disagrees with some of the clauses, then it may cause a vacancy because they aren't interested in renting the property anymore. Having a well-written lease agreement will help deter problems such as anyone signing a lease when there is already another person on the rental property that is notifying them that they are moving out.

Asking for a big security deposit: A landlord can ask for a big security deposit to discourage anyone from breaking the rules of the lease agreement. This can help improve the reputation and safety of the property in order to keep it less likely for a tenant to move out. The landlord can also waive a portion or all of their security deposit if they do not want to use it because they don't want to risk losing potential tenants.

How to Advertise your Property Correctly

Rental listings websites such as Craigslist and eBay offer unique opportunities to advertise your investment property. Below you will find some tips to market your property effectively:

Make your contact details easy to find: Including information about how to contact you in the listing is a good way to make your listing stand out. For example, put your street address or local postcode, city, state, and zip code where it's easy to find on the listing. You should include a phone number so prospective tenants can contact you easily.

Take a few high-quality pictures: It is very important to invest in photography. Take a few high- quality photos of your rental property so that people are able to fully visualize what the inside looks like from different angles and perspectives. Professional images aren't required; however, having 3-5 high-quality photos can assist.

Add details about your amenities: You can include information about the amenities of your property to make the listing more interesting. This can include the number of bedrooms and bathrooms, parking availability, remodeling work that has been done or is going to be done to the property, and anything else that you think would be appealing to people.

Use relevant keywords: If you want your property to be found through a search, then using relevant words is vital. In your listing, include descriptions of your property in bullet points and, ideally, use a keyword-rich title for the listing. Also, remember to include a description of what is included in the rental (e.g.: 'brand new home').

Create events: It is important to create events and invite people to them so as to promote your property. Make sure that you include a link to the event so that people can RSVP and attend it. If you are hosting events on your property, add this to the listing. For example, if you have a cook-off in your home, list this on the listing, so there is an opportunity for others to see it.

Make your listing as appealing as possible: You want to add as much information about your property as possible and make it easy for people to find specific details they are looking for. You don't have to write a complete guide on how to use the property but make it easy for people to figure out the specifics of what they are looking for.

Use social media ads: Social media is an effective marketing channel to reach people. You can create Facebook and Instagram ads that will be shown to people who are inappropriate demographics for the property. This is a good method of reaching the right audience, so consider setting up these ads to advertise your rental listing.

Consider technology: If you are a DIY kind of person, then you may want to consider technology such as indoor/outdoor cameras and sensors for your property. For example, you can set up sensors so that you are notified when someone enters or exits the house. This may not be necessary, but it is a thought to consider, and this kind of technology has been proven to reduce crime in the property as well.

Importance of high-quality photos for rental properties

In today's day and age, landlords have found the importance of having quality photos in their rental properties. This can be either through a professional photographer or by taking the time to learn how to take your own quality photos. There are many benefits of having high-quality photos rather than generic ones, such as improving search rates and increasing the price that you can ask for your unit. Some benefits of having high- quality photos of your property when advertising is explained below:

Increased traffic: With the internet being one of the most used tools in our current society, having professional photos will increase traffic. Having quality pictures will show that you are a serious landlord and that your property is worth viewing. As well, because it is important to have photos that are high quality, people who are viewing your listing are more likely to make an inquiry as they can trust in seeing what they will be renting.

Display identity of your property: The identity of your property is a crucial part of the renting process. With high-quality photos, you can showcase the look, feel, and design of your unit, as well as any features that make it stand out. This allows potential renters to see what they will be renting in their minds before they look at it or during their inspection.

Builds credibility: Because you can use high-quality photos to showcase your rental property, potential renters and/or buyers will trust that they are seeing what they are getting when they make an inquiry. This will build credibility in your listing as potential renters know that you have provided quality photos of the property and have the best intentions for their renting experience.

Increases property value: Having high-quality photos of your rental property will increase the value that you are asking for your property. With a high-quality photo, potential renters will see the value in what they are getting and its condition before making an inquiry. This will increase the price that you can ask for your unit as well as improve your chances of receiving a higher offer.

High-quality photos make your website easy to navigate: High-quality photos allow potential renters to easily navigate through your website, as well as allow potential sellers to search for properties that are within their price range. This will help potential buyers and renters find what they are looking for with ease and make it easy for them to decide whether or not your property is what they want.

Produces faster results: High-quality photos will produce faster results when the person making an inquiry is searching for a property. When people are searching for a property or conducting a search on an online listing, they want to know that they are seeing what they will be renting and that the picture is high quality. With high- quality photos, potential renters do not have to take their time looking through every listing, as it will be clear which listings are high quality.

Chapter 6:

Dealing with Tenant Problems

As a landlord, whether you're dealing with petty vandalism, theft of property, or a tenant who needs help getting along with his neighbors, there are several important points you should take into account. In all these situations, there's no need to have any delay or confusion in your decisions. No matter what you do, it is always a very good idea to ensure that you are following the law.

The Tenants' Rights Act is a state law that states that tenants must follow the terms of their lease, which can include whether or not to pay for utilities and how much to pay. The law does not define "illegal alterations" or what should be done if your tenant decides to make such alterations. The law also doesn't spell out exactly what constitutes "illegal actions."

"In general, you are free to decide whether or not your tenant is following the lease agreement," said Stephanie K. Lewis, executive director of the Metropolitan Boston Housing Partnership. "But if you are going to take any action against your tenant, it's always a good idea to follow the law. The law is a good guide for what you can do and what you should not do in terms of evicting or charging your tenant."

Tenants are allowed to have pets, but these animals may cause problems with the rest of the tenants. For example, if a cat pees in one of the neighbor's apartments, it can be considered a violation. If your tenant is not following the terms of the lease and refuses to remove the animal, it's best to call the authorities because you may be violating your tenant's rights.

If your tenant is causing trouble for other tenants, you can take action by calling in the authorities or filing an eviction notice. The state law doesn't explain what to do if you suspect that your tenant is dealing with an illegal substance such as drugs or if he's involved in illegal trafficking of any kind. If a tenant is dealing drugs, there are separate laws that apply.

The penalties for illegal alterations or other illegal actions are the same as if you yourself were involved in them. In order to prevent such actions, it's best to remain vigilant and keep track of what your tenant is doing. It's also important to make sure that your tenant is not doing anything illegal on the premises and make sure he doesn't violate any of your rights as a landlord.

To avoid having trouble with your tenants, the best step to take is to establish good communication between yourself and the tenants. It's always a good idea to make sure that your tenant understands the rules and agrees to follow them. This is particularly important when it comes to repairs, rules about pets, and utilities.

How To Have Effective Communication With Your Tenants

Every property owner has heard horror stories about trying to communicate with their tenants. The worst communication problems are when the tenant fails to pay rent on time or tries to skip out without cleaning up after themselves. But even worse are the situations that arise when there's little chance of reaching a mutually satisfying resolution. The following are some tips to boost effective communication with your tenants:

Be Professional and Respectful: At the start of any interaction with your tenants, it's important to maintain a friendly, professional attitude. Asking your tenants if they have any questions or concerns is a good way to start.

This can be achieved either through meeting in person or over a phone call, which is easier said than done when dealing with some of the most difficult tenant problems. Ask for their signature on a lease agreement and ask them to show you the apartment before signing anything. This will allow you to get their feedback on how well they feel the lease meets their needs and expectations. Make sure that everything is clear and grammatically correct before you give them their copy. There are many other things to consider when drafting a lease too. Being respectful to your tenants brings them closer to you, and they know they can rely on you. They will be more willing to work out their issues with you, and the problems will usually go away without the need for any legal action.

Write Everything Down: Writing things down will help you get your point across if you're dealing with a tenant that is a lousy communicator or doesn't use strong communication skills. If a tenant delays in paying their rent, writing it down and sending them an email or even a text message helps them to be sure that they understand your concern about being late with the rent. Creating an email account for your properties can be helpful in staying on top of your communication with multiple tenants. It allows you to send out important notices and updates to your tenants without the worry of misplacing something or sending it to the wrong email address. Writing everything down also helps you to keep the tone of your message polite and professional. Even if you are dealing with someone who is trying to push your buttons, writing it down and sending it back to them in email forces you to be respectful.

Always Keep the Communication Lines Open: Having open communication with your tenants is a good way to ensure that they know exactly what's expected of them and when they are able to expect their rent payments. It also gives you a way to smooth things over when there are problems with the rent or any other issue. If you are unable to reach your tenant by phone, it's a good idea to send them an email or a text message so you don't miss out on sending important information to them. Tenants with more difficult issues will often be less likely to respond if they think that it will cause them trouble.

Keeping the communication lines open will help to ensure that you can reach them with any new information.

Be as Flexible as Possible: If you are dealing with a tenant who is struggling to stay on top of their rent or some other issue, it's important to be flexible with them. Understanding their situation and working out ways to give them a bit more time or wiggle room can help to keep the lines of communication open. If they are paying their rent on time and keeping the property clean and well maintained, there's no reason not to. Asking your tenant if they are having any problems with the rent before it's due can also help you to understand their situation. It will give them an opportunity to let you know if there is an issue or if they have arranged a way of paying the rent. Creating payment plans with your tenants can also be helpful in a number of different situations. If you are dealing with a tenant struggling to pay the rent, a payment plan might help them pay the rent on time each month. Asking them to make smaller direct deposits into your account separately can also be helpful when dealing with tenants who normally pay their rent together. This will allow them to make each payment independently, and you won't have to worry about receiving all of the money at once.

Don't show up unannounced: If you are dealing with a tenant who is struggling to stay on top of the rent, it's usually a good idea to call and let them know that you will be paying them a visit. If they aren't expecting your visit, it can create unnecessary stress and foster bad feelings between you and the tenant. Another reason why it's important not to show up unannounced when dealing with tenants is that it puts them on edge. Tenants who are afraid might try to hide things from you or become angry and defensive. Remember that you have the right to take a look at your property. If you are worried that something in the apartment might be broken or that they are not taking proper care of it, it's important to be able to see what is happening and make a visit. Tenants who are hiding things from you are not being honest and fair. If you think that they might be afraid or angry when you show up, let them know in advance when you might be visiting.

Letting them know that it's important to keep the lines of communication open will usually make them more amenable to your visit.

Keep a List of Emergency Contacts: When dealing with tenants who have special needs or disabilities, it's a good idea to get their emergency contact information. If you have a tenant who is unable to pay their rent or who becomes unable to care for their property due to a medical issue, it's important to have the contact information of someone who can help them. If the tenant starts having any issues with the property, the emergency contact will be able to take over responsibility. Looking through your copy of your lease agreement can help you find out what type of information you need. If you enter the name and contact information of someone who can take over if the tenant is unable to pay their rent, be sure to include that person's address and phone number in your listing. If you don't know what type of emergency contact information you need, it's a good idea to check your lease agreement or go through with your property manager. They should be able to help you locate your copy of the lease agreement and any other important documents from which you need to get this information.

Remember that we're all human: When you are dealing with tenants who are struggling to pay their rent or another issue, it's important to remember that everyone makes mistakes. There may be multiple reasons why they are struggling, and they deserve a chance to explain what is happening with their finances. Avoiding the situation won't help to fix the problem but being nice and understanding can help you reach an agreement that keeps you both happy. Tenants who are suffering financial difficulties are unlikely to be insulted if you question their situation. It can be useful to let your property manager know when you're dealing with tenants who have special needs or disabilities because they might have a better understanding of the situation than you. It's important that you don't give up on your tenant if you discover that they are having financial issues. There are lots of things that they might need to do to get back on their feet, and it's your responsibility to help them as much as possible.

Being kind and understanding when dealing with a tenant who is having financial issues will help you reach an agreement that both parties can live with.

How to Handle Late Payment of Rent

Tenant delays in paying rent are a fairly common occurrence, and there are a number of options for landlords who have tenants with this difficulty. The first option is to grant a tenant a short-term extension on their rental payments. This can be done by helping the tenant establish a plan to pay off the balance. Landlords should always make sure to receive some form of payment before agreeing to an extension and have the tenant sign an agreement that states the terms and conditions of the deal, including how long it will last and what will happen if they miss a payment again.

When dealing with a tenant who has a history of not paying

rent on time, some landlords choose to give the tenant a notice to move out. This can be done if the landlord has already given the tenant multiple notices that their rent is late, and they have failed to pay rent after an appropriate grace period. Some states may require that the landlord has attempted to evict or file an unlawful detainer before being able to give the notice to leave, but some states don't require this.

But before taking the above steps, it is important for a landlord to follow a certain procedure, which is outlined below:

Check your lease documents and payment records: If a tenant delays in paying their rent, landlords should check their lease to see if any provisions have been made for this. If there are none, then the landlord should review their payment records so they can figure out when the next due date will be. If you have a record of when the tenant has not paid rent on time in the past, this is important so you can look at how often they delayed payments. Checking your lease documents also helps confirm that the tenant is truly late with their payment.

The landlord should also check whether there are any late fees specified in their lease. If so, they should make it clear to the tenant that they will be charged these fees due to their delay.

Send a late rent notice: If the tenant is late on rent, and the landlord has tried unsuccessfully to communicate with them about it, then the landlord should send a letter to the tenant. This gives them a chance to make an attempt at making their payment. If the tenant delays in paying their rent after this notice is sent, then the landlord should file a lawsuit for back rent. This gives them a chance to take the tenant to court and have the judge issue a ruling on their case. It is important for the landlord to make sure that they clearly explain what is happening in their letter and that they include information about when they sent the late rent notice and temporary storage fees should they be able to get back any of their possession.

Try making a phone call to the tenant: Most landlords have found that making a phone call to the tenant and explaining the situation will work much better. This gives them an opportunity to get the tenant to resolve their late payment in a more reasonable manner. Many times, tenants are willing to do it for free in order for them to keep their rental property and not go out of business because of a bad lease contract. The landlord should always be clear when they are making the call and what will happen if they continue with their problem after making this call.

Send a pay or quit notice: Following the phone call or after they have sent the late rent notice, landlords can send a pay or quit notice letter to their tenant. This gives them a final chance to make their rent payment before the landlord initiates an eviction action against them. If this is done, the landlord

140

should be sure to include all relevant information about when the rent was due and how much it was supposed to be for. The landlord should also clearly state that if the tenant does not pay in full within ten days, then they will file a lawsuit for rent in due course.

Take legal action: Declaring that the tenant's rent is due and owing and taking them to court is a very common step for a landlord to take. If the tenant defaults in paying their rent, then the landlord could either file for unlawful detainer and force them out of their property or ask the judge to issue an eviction order that allows them to force the tenant out of their home. Either way, it will give the landlord more control over their rental property. However, it is critical for landlords to obey the state's eviction procedures and regulations. If the landlord decides to take legal action, he or she will be required to pay fees and fill some paperwork out to get the eviction proceedings going. The landlord should make sure that they are able to pay the fees because the court will not release them from this situation, and it is important for them to have this lawsuit completed properly.

Action to Take When Your Tenant has Illegal Drugs

Many landlords are worried about what to do when their tenant has illegal drugs in the home. Drug possession is a criminal offense, and there are many tenants who have been arrested for drug possession while they lived on their landlord's property. This is something that every landlord should take into consideration when dealing with tenants who have substances such as marijuana and heroin on the premises.

About ten years ago, New York State made possession of less than a half-ounce of marijuana a criminal violation. With this law in effect, a landlord has the right to evict and/or move out any tenant who has more than a half-ounce of marijuana.

This section gives an overview of what landlords should do if they find their tenants in possession of illegal drugs:

Document everything: If the police are involved in the search, a landlord has a duty to document everything that happened. The police will most likely seize any evidence in the home, and this can include things such as fingerprints, digital videos, and any other material documentation that may be helpful to an investigation.

Once an investigation is complete, both the landlord and tenant will have copies of any vital records. Landlords should also document the search and any other circumstances that might have caused a change in the tenant's behavior. This could include sudden circumstances such as death, divorce, or any health problems that might have occurred. It is also important to document other tenants' reports on the issue as well as records of unusual utility bills.

Talk to an attorney: The best thing a landlord can do is consult an attorney who concentrates on real estate law. When a tenant is arrested for drug possession, a landlord must do everything in their power to evict the tenant.

Many times, this involves using their attorney as well as any other possible resources they have available to them. A good lawyer will explain all of the legal complications associated with an eviction and what type of evidence needs to be presented as well as what can be done in order to get the tenant out of the property as quickly and efficiently as possible.

Contact the Police: If the renter is still in possession of drugs, the landlord should inform the police station in his or her neighborhood. It is usually advisable to contact the police before anything happens, and if there is a possibility that an arrest may occur, it makes sense to take small steps to prevent any issues before they happen. To avoid any issues with the police, a landlord should make sure they explain that they suspect illegal activity and haven't actually witnessed it. When contacting the police, a landlord needs to be very clear in explaining what they have observed. This is important because a police officer may ask a tenant question regarding their behavior. If the officer asks why the landlord thinks they would do something illegal, and the landlord just says, "Well, they always seem to do things like this," then that landlord will most likely be charged with obstruction of justice. To avoid these situations, be as detailed as possible and remember that it is better to have a police officer ask you a few questions than to be arrested on a drug possession charge.

File an eviction lawsuit: If the tenant is on the property illegally or has been arrested, a landlord will need to file an eviction lawsuit in the local court. The landlord should make sure they obtain copies of any legal documents that they have signed and keep them in a safe place. If a tenant is not on the property, a landlord will have to find proof of abandonment. There are various ways that this can be done, and it depends on the state in which the landlord lives. In New York, the landlord must make sure they follow the rules set by New York State regarding abandonment. If there has been any reasonable cause for termination of tenancy, then an eviction lawsuit will be successful without having to file any additional steps.

These causes can vary from state to state, and some of the most important concerns are the landlord's right to sell or rent the property any lease violations or damages caused to the right. When an eviction lawsuit is successful, a tenant has five days to vacate the premises. At this point, a landlord must make sure they have contacted their local police department and hired a local bail bondsman in order to remove them from the property as quickly and efficiently as possible.

Action to Take When Your Tenant Dies

If you own a rental property, you may be wondering what to do if one of your tenants dies. If the tenant was on a month-to-month rental agreement and all parties involved agreed to monthly payments, there is no need to take any action. If the tenant was on a lease agreement or all parties involved agreed to quarterly payments, you will need to take some steps in order for the estate's executor or family members to make arrangements with their bank.

Rental agreements and lease agreements are legally binding contracts. Even if you do not want to continue the tenancy with a member of the tenant's family, you may not break the terms of the contract without consequences. If you decide to evict a deceased tenant's estate or family from your property, it is important that all parties involved are aware that breaking a rental agreement can result in both civil and criminal liability for you.

Rental contracts typically have clauses about what happens when a tenant dies. If they do, you will need to follow the lease or rental agreement's policies. Before you start any eviction process, talk to the landlord-tenant attorney and review both your state's laws and your rental contract. Below are some steps a landlord can take if their tenant dies:

Obtain a written notice of your tenant's death: The landlord should obtain a written notice of the tenant's death. If the deceased tenant's family members are living on the same property, you will need to obtain a certified copy of their death certificate. If not, you will need to obtain proof from a local law enforcement agency indicating that a body was found in the apartment and that it has been identified as your tenant.

After you have the death notice, write a letter to your tenant's executor or other family members informing them of the tenant's death if they do not reside in the same property. Make sure that you include a copy of the death certificate and any other relevant information. Let the person know that you will be taking possession of their belongings and ask them to contact you if they need assistance.

Letter Example:

"It is with the deepest regret that I am writing to inform you that your father has passed away. On (month/day/year), he was found unconscious in his apartment and taken to the hospital, where he was pronounced dead. An autopsy into his death is underway, but it is believed that cardiac arrest or a heart attack was the primary cause of death. Your father named (name and address of your property) as his estate's executor, which means that I will be responsible for assisting you with any matters relating to your father's death."

You may also need to inform local law enforcement agencies that the lease or rental agreement has been terminated. The family members will need to obtain a death certificate and learn if they are responsible for paying rent and other related expenses. If there are no other tenants living in the apartment, you may be able to evict your tenant's estate from the property without an attorney.

Secure the Property: If your tenant is deceased, you will need to secure the apartment or house. You do not want anyone else accessing the premises and removing any property that belongs to the deceased tenant. Lock all of the apartment or house's doors and windows, but remember to make sure that you leave a way for any family members who may need access to their belongings.

Make arrangements for your tenant's belongings: All of the property left behind by the deceased tenant (or an executor if the estate has been opened) needs to be removed. Generally speaking, you are not responsible for disposing of any personal property left in the apartment or house in accordance with your local laws and ordinances. You will need to decide on a fair way to divide up any remaining personal property between yourself and the family members who do not reside on your property. The executor of the deceased tenant's estate or family members may make arrangements to get rid of any remaining property outside of your property. Make sure you have confirmation that the estate of the dead renter was removed from your property. You may also be required to take pictures and keep a logbook or other records of the estate's removal and storage.

Deal with The Lease: If your tenant was on a lease, you would have to find a way to remove the lease from your property. If you are in one of the states where a deceased tenant's estate can surrender the lease, there is generally no need to contact your real estate attorney. If your tenant's estate is unable to surrender the lease, consider letting them out of it by returning their security deposit. Remember, however, that the lease is a legally binding contract, and you may be held responsible for unpaid rent if you evict the tenant's estate without following your lease's terms.

How to Handle Your Property Being Abandoned

If you own rental property, you're likely aware that tenants can simply just decide to leave. If this happens, it's not always as easy as it sounds. When things go wrong, everyone's emotions can run high, and it's important to keep your cool. So, how do you handle a tenant that has abandoned your property?

You're renting out your property, and the tenant packs their stuff into boxes and leaves a note telling you they've decided to vacate the unit. Now what? Well, luckily, there are plenty of ways to deal with this situation.

Make sure they really are gone: Ensure that the tenant really has left the property and they are not just hiding out. It could be a busy time of year; maybe they are waiting for a new place to move in, so check your records and make sure this is really happening. You can find out if they are really gone by checking the records to see if they are still paying rent. If they've stopped, check with your property manager to see if they have an excuse. Another important thing to do is talk to their emergency contacts. If they are missing, you can check with these people to see if they've heard from the tenant and find out where they are. Talking to the neighbors can also be helpful in this situation because they might have some useful information about their whereabouts. You can also give the tenant a notice of inspection of the property. If there is no response, you can check the property and inspect the utilities to confirm if they are really gone.

Document Your Investigation: If you believe that the tenant has left because of a problem with the property, you should document your investigation. You can present this to the city and other people involved in the process to ensure that no one is taking advantage of the situation.

You should also take pictures and have a record of what happened and what notations about any problems or damages. Ensure that you are tracking all addresses that your tenant provided if you need to send them notice or make arrangements for them after they leave. You can also record conversations with your tenant to see if they are trying to duck out of the lease. Make sure that you've told everyone involved in the process, so you have a record of who did what and when. You should also preserve a copy of the notice of departure and verify the property for any notices from the renter after they have left. Always make a note of any contact information that they have in case you need to contact them or if there is ever an issue with their apartment after they leave.

Send the Tenant a Notice of Abandonment: If you think that you have an abandoned property, then it's time to send the tenant a notice of abandonment. This notice should be sent within the first 60 days after they had left and should state when their last rent payment was made. This is important for you because it can give you leverage in court if there are disputes about who or what caused them to abandon the property. It's also good for you to note that if you send them a notice of abandonment within the first month, then you can decide to file an eviction or put their property out on the street. If you wait until after the first month, then your only option will be to take them to court. The notice should include very detailed information about the notice and how you are going to be dealing with the property, including a timeline of what is going to happen. It should list all of their contacts if they want to dispute it. The notice should also include a demand for the tenant to respond and statements about who is responsible for the cost of repairs if any are needed.

Terminate the Lease: The easiest way to deal with a tenant who has abandoned the property is to terminate their lease. You will need the tenant's signature, and you should get this in writing. If they are not in agreement, then you should get a court order for them to sign their lease. This is something that will have to be done in court before you can legally terminate their lease for abandonment. You should take these steps very seriously and ensure that you are following all the requirements of your lease. You need to get permission from your tenants as well as all other parties involved in the lease, such as your property manager or broker. You could also ask an attorney if they have any questions because it is important that you do this correctly and legally. If you decide to terminate the lease, then make sure it's done properly. You need to make sure that the lease termination is being done correctly. You must also make certain that you are following all local rules and laws. You should also make sure you have not deprived them of any of their rights.

Chapter 7:

Aligning Yourself with Fair Housing

Understanding Fair Housing

Fair housing is the policy of providing equal access to housing opportunities. It is a legal term that covers not just physical access to housing- but also non-physical factors such as access to services and social activities, shared community spaces, and information on job opportunities. Many believe race and class are major factors in determining fair housing in the United States.

There are many issues that concern fair housing.

Discrimination is a key issue in most areas of fair housing focuses on. Discrimination means any action or decision made by a landlord or other housing professional that excludes any living unit (apartment, house, etc.) or household based on the perceived race, color, religion, or national origin (also called ancestry). Discrimination may be intentional or unintentional.

Another issue involved in fair housing is equal opportunity. Equal opportunity refers to the policy of providing a level playing field for all citizens when it comes to housing, regardless of race or class. All citizens should be treated fairly and equally when they are applying for or trying to rent or purchase a home or apartment unit. Equal opportunity in housing also includes many community services and activities (such as parks, stores, schools, accepting special education programs).

The Fair Housing Act (FHAct) is the most important piece of legislation that enforces fair housing. The FHAct was passed on April 11, 1968, by Richard Nixon and covered both buyers and renters.

A person can file a complaint with HUD (Department of Housing and Urban Development) if they feel they are not being treated well when applying or attempting to rent or purchase housing in their area.

A landlord or other housing professional is not legally allowed to refuse to rent or lease a unit, house, or apartment based on race, color, religion, national origin (also called ancestry), and sex. Discrimination can also be expressed as discrimination by action toward one person on the basis of his/her race, color, religion or nationality.

HUD has a Fair Housing Testing Program (FHTP) that "exposes discrimination in the rental and sale of dwellings. HUD testing is conducted by specially trained fair housing testers who pose as renters or buyers and visit apartment complexes, individual properties, or real estate offices to determine if there are discriminatory policies or procedures being followed."

A landlord is legally allowed to evict a tenant for not paying rent or breaching the agreement in most states. The exception to this is if the tenant's payment issue is due to the landlord violating fair housing law. Failure to fix a broken bathroom, for example, would be a violation of fair housing law, and therefore the tenant would not be required to pay rent until the landlord fixed the problem.

Rules to Make Sure You are Under Fair Housing

Landlords often find themselves violating fair housing laws either knowingly or unknowingly. When a landlord illegally discriminates against a tenant, they can be sued and ordered to pay damages to the victim in the amount of actual and punitive damages. Here are some pointers to assist landlords in avoiding unintentional tenant discrimination.

Create rules that treat tenants with children the same as those without children: It is unacceptable for a landlord to discriminate against tenants with children. No landlord may refuse to rent a unit or charge an additional rent because of family status. When a landlord is asked to abide by laws and regulations that are already in place, it is very important for them to understand their responsibilities as well as the rights of their tenants. As a result of this Act, it is imperative for landlords to put in place rules and policies which are fair and applied equally across all tenants regardless of size and household composition.

Retain proper documentation of a prospective tenant's application process: It is crucial for a landlord to document the entire process of screening prospective tenants, including the application and review process. It can be helpful to include all the terms and conditions of renting a property in the lease. This way, tenants know what they must do in order to maintain their tenancy status. Landlords should make sure that they have considered all aspects of fairness during this process, such as requiring equal income from both tenants and reference checks from their employer or previous landlords. Retaining these documents is also important in the event the landlord is accused of going against fair housing rules. The landlord must also include a copy of the lease agreement in this file, as well as an explanation detailing how the tenant can make a complaint.

Accept rental application except if the prospective tenant does not meet your qualification criteria: It is a common myth among landlords that they have the right to turn away potential tenants. If you are only accepting tenants based on income or refusing to rent to applicants based on the tenant's age, you are in violation of the federal Fair Housing

Act. This law protects all those who wish to rent from being discriminated against because of their family status or race. Landlords should ensure that any policies or rules which they set forth are fair and apply equally to all tenants. This way, they can always maintain their status as a law-abiding landlord and avoid running into unnecessary problems in the future.

Do not make inquiries about family information of the prospective tenant: It is illegal for landlords to ask about a tenant's familial status, the number of children, and if any of the children have disabilities. Questions such as the number of children and the age of children may be considered discriminatory if they are not asked of all tenants. Landlords should remember that it is their job to screen applicants and ensure that only qualified tenants are accepted into the property. It means that any preliminary questions should be kept to a minimum which can help reduce unnecessary conflicts or disruptions in the future between landlord and tenant.

Do not disclose information about the tenant to other tenants: As a landlord, you may feel as if you are not doing anything wrong by disclosing information about your tenant. It is quite common for landlords to contact their neighbors or their other tenants and ask them about the individual who is renting. The issue with this is that it may negatively affect the renter who is renting from you. The landlord's neighbor may feel as if there is a problem between the landlord and the tenant, and this can lead to an uncomfortable situation. It is also important for landlords to realize that they are not required to discuss their tenants with other tenants.

Do not deny a disabled tenant's request for an assigned parking spot: The Fair Housing Act not only prohibits landlords from discriminating against disabled persons but also requires them to make reasonable accommodations for their needs. This includes giving a disabled tenant an assigned parking spot near their unit. Landlords should remember that they are not allowed to use any sort of disability as a reason to deny a tenant from renting from you. Instead, you must consider all tenants in an even manner and attempt to accommodate their needs through reasonable means. Embarking on this type of action may reflect negatively on your reputation and can lead to legal trouble. As a landlord, you should remember that you may be required to provide parking spots for those who have disabilities or may require an assigned parking spot for the future. You must not only provide these reasonable accommodations but ensure that the tenants are comfortable and safe when using the spaces.

Do not evict a hoarder: It is illegal for landlords to evict or terminate a tenant due to hoarding. Hoarding is considered a disability. There are also other laws that are considered to be preemptive laws that protect tenants with hoarding disorder as well as other disordered behavior. Hoarding disorder can be defined by the excessive collection and keeping of objects which may have no apparent value to others. Landlords must be very careful about evicting a tenant for hoarding behavior. If you do, you could face hefty charges under the Fair Housing Act. You might also anticipate being sued by the renter who was evicted in this manner. A landlord should remember that before evictions happen, they should work with their tenants to come up with a reasonable solution to this problem. The tenant should understand that they are not allowed to hoard other people's belongings, and they must adhere to a set of rules. If eviction is the only option, a landlord may want to use an outside party like a social worker or psychologist to try and help the tenant come up with solutions. There are also support organizations that can assist tenants in learning how to deal with hoarding and making plans for eviction if necessary.

Establish a clear maintenance policy: It is very important for a landlord to establish a clear maintenance policy. This can help to reduce conflicts between you and your tenants. You should be able to do this by making sure that you outline everything in writing and make sure that you have policies that are fair for both you and the tenant. One of the most important things you should do is to clearly state your maintenance policy and make sure that it is something that everyone can sign on to. It helps you and the tenant to be aware of what is expected from everyone. If you are not sure where to start, try using a sample maintenance policy that will help you get started. Another thing that you need to do as a landlord is to make sure that your maintenance crew and any subcontractors are provided with proper training and information. This way, they will be able to maintain the premises properly, and you will not have to make any other decisions in the future. You should make sure that the maintenance crew and subcontractors are aware of how to properly deal with issues such as mold, termites, rodents, and fire hazards. You need to also make sure that they are equipped with all necessary equipment, evidence preservation, and safety protocols. Once you have established a maintenance policy, it is best that you enforce it on your tenants as well.

Provide Fair Housing Training to all Your Staff or Employees

As a landlord, it is only fair that you equip the employees working on your property with fair housing knowledge and skills through proper training. This can help you protect your employees and will help ensure that your tenants' Fair Housing Rights are not violated. You need to make sure that your employees are made aware of their responsibilities and know how to deal with issues such as harassment and discrimination properly. You need to train all of your staff, be they management, maintenance, or housekeeping workers. Training should be done at the time that someone is first hired by you and should then be repeated annually. You want to make sure that your employees are aware of what they are legally allowed to say and do so they do not make any false or inaccurate statements, which can damage your reputation.

Examples of Fair Housing Discrimination

Fair Housing discrimination happens on a very wide scale. This section gives some examples of housing discrimination:

Refusing to Rent Out to Immigrants: In 2006, a landlord in El Monte refused to rent out a house to an immigrant couple because they were Mexican. This is an example of fair housing discrimination based on national origin. It is unfair, illegal, and morally wrong. California Fair Employment and Housing (FEHA) enforces laws that deal with discrimination based on national origin. The goal of this law is to make sure everyone has equal opportunities when it comes to housing. Landlords are also not allowed to assume someone's nationality by the way they look or by their name.

Refusing to Rent Out to Families With Children: In 2012, a landlord in San Marcos refused to rent out the property to a family with children. This is another example of fair housing discrimination based on familial status. This kind of discrimination is also known as familial status discrimination.

Fair housing protects families with children from being discriminated against when renting or buying housing. When renting or buying a home, there should ideally be no restrictions on the number of children allowed in the household. This act is intended to prevent landlords from refusing to rent out a property to families with children because they think the children will be noisy or because they don't want children around. This act also protects mothers who are pregnant or have newborn babies from being discriminated against while they are pregnant or after their babies are born. This act is a very important law that helps protect families with young children from being discriminated against on the basis of familial status.

Refusing to Rent Out to Black People or other racial groups: In 2008, two African-American couples were rejected by a landlord based on their race. This is an example of unfair housing discrimination based on race or color. A landlord should not be allowed to reject a black or Hispanic person because he believes that he would be unfit for living in the area or because he wants to avoid potential problems. This is clearly racism and unfair housing discrimination. It is also a very serious crime that can lead to large fines for the landlord. It is possible that the landlord would also be forced to pay damages to the black, Hispanic, or Asian person whom he denied housing. There are laws against this kind of racism and unfair housing discrimination. The Civil Rights Act of 1968 safeguards persons from racial discrimination. The Fair Housing Act gives a person the right to live in any neighborhood they want to live in regardless of race, color, gender, or disability. Additionally, the Fair Housing Act allows a person to sue a landlord if they feel that they were treated unfairly or discriminated against by a landlord who refused to rent out property based on race.

Some states have harsher penalties for violations of this law. Most states have laws against discriminating against people based on race and color.

Housing Discrimination Based on Sexual Orientation: In 2013, a landlord in San Francisco refused to rent out a property to a gay couple because he wanted to avoid potential problems with his other tenants. The Fair Housing Act forbids discrimination against renters and potential renters on the basis of their sexual orientation or gender identity, among other factors. For example, a landlord should not be able to refuse to rent out a property because he doesn't want potential tenants who are gay or lesbian. This act is also known as sexual orientation discrimination.

Refusing to Rent Out to a Veteran and his Family: In 2012, a landlord in Merced refused to rent out a property to an Iraq War Veteran and his wife because he didn't want veterans living in the neighborhood. This is an example of fair housing discrimination based on veteran status. Landlords cannot refuse to rent out a property because they feel that veterans may be noisy or cause trouble in the neighborhood. This is clearly unfair treatment of military service members and veterans who have done their jobs for our country. It can also be devastating to a veteran who has lost a loved one during war. The Fair Housing Act seeks to protect veterans and those who have served in the military from discrimination when renting or buying housing. It also protects their right to have access to housing that is equal and safe for them. The Fair Housing Act says that no one should be treated in a way that denies them any civil rights because of their military service.

Refusing to Rent Out Property to a Person with a Disability: In 2005, a landlord in West Hollywood refused to rent out a property to a person with a disability. This is an example of fair housing discrimination based on disability. A landlord should not be allowed to refuse to rent out a property to someone just because they have a disability. The Fair Housing Act protects people against discrimination based on disabilities when renting or buying housing. However, there are other circumstances where a person's disability can be considered a reason to refuse to rent out a property. A landlord should not be allowed to refuse to rent out property just because he thinks that disabled tenants are noisy or will cause trouble in the neighborhood.

The Importance of Fair Housing

There are many different laws that have been created to ensure those who do not have the same opportunities due to the color of their skin are not discriminated against. The laws state that it is illegal for any person or organization, such as a bank, real estate company, or other business enterprises, to discriminate in any aspect of housing transactions.

Fair housing laws are set up to ensure all races can have a fair opportunity at purchasing or renting property. It is a federal law that requires all owners, property managers, and other affiliated individuals to look at housing prospects from the perspective of an integrated society. Fair housing laws do not allow an owner to write or make any kind of statement that shows that they are racially biased with their decisions. They also do not allow a real estate agent to refuse to list, show or sell a home based on the race of the person who wants to purchase it.

Throughout the years, many people have tried to stop the movement of fair housing laws. They believe that it is unfair for there to be laws promoting racial integration, believing that it would cause problems with those who are racist. Some of these people tried to find ways of stopping racial integration in both the north and south by-passing laws restricting such movements. For example, in the South, a law was passed known as Jim Crow Laws or "Black Codes," which were put in place shortly after slavery was abolished. These laws were set up to prevent blacks from buying property. When the Jim Crow Laws did not work, those who wanted to stop integration resorted to violence. In order for someone to buy property, it was necessary for them to have enough money, be a white man, and be married. If any of these requirements were met, the property might be transferred with little opposition.

In a lot of states, there have been cases where blacks and whites fought at that time over the spread of fair housing laws. The Civil Rights Act of 1968 was created to end housing discrimination. The law states that a person cannot question a home buyer or renter about their financial status and that they must be considered for the property regardless of their skin color. Since the Civil Rights Act of 1968, there have been many cases where people have been tried for breaking fair housing laws.

These cases were made to ensure that fair housing stays an ongoing procedure and that it is not just a law on paper.

The creation of fair housing laws has come with many advantages, especially for minority groups all across our country.

Without fair housing, decisions on where to live are often made based on things like a neighborhood's racial makeup and the race of people who live in that neighborhood. With fair housing laws, you can find a place to feel safe and comfortable regardless of your skin color.

A person should be able to rent or buy a home without having to deal with extra red tape. Often, areas and buildings that are predominantly minority groups are targeted by real estate agents who try to sell them homes in an area where they may not fit in.

Minority groups are often targeted for housing loans that have high-interest rates, predatory home loans, and sometimes outright fraud. A lot of minority families do not have the financial stability to take advantage of home- ownership opportunities because of situations like these.

The Fair Housing Act gives people from all walks of life the opportunity to purchase a home without being discriminated against. It also protects them from any illegal situations, such as intimidation and threats of violence.

Fair housing laws have helped the black and white communities come together and have helped many people gain a better life without fear of being homeless or having a hard time getting an apartment of their own.

Penalties for Going against Fair Housing

There is no enemy more sinister than ignorance and discrimination to stand against in our society today, especially when it comes to housing policies. When a person with a disability, a black, Hispanic, or Asian person, gets denied a home loan or apartment, you don't see the same kind of outrage from other races to protect their rights. Not only are these people denied housing, but they are also drawn into litigation lawsuits and harassed by unruly police officers. Below are some of the penalties landlords may face if they are found guilty of violating fair housing laws:

The landlord may be charged by the US Department of Housing and Urban Development: In this instance, the landlord may be forced to attend several hearings and defend themselves from the allegations. This may also be worse for the landlord because the US Department of Justice may decide to pursue the case further on behalf of the tenant.

The landlord will have to compensate the tenant or prospective tenant for damages: In this scenario, the landlord must pay the tenant damages of up to $100,000 and/or receive a license suspension. In addition, the landlord may also be subjected to a multi-million dollar fine charged by HUD for violating fair housing laws.

The landlord may also be forced to pay non- economic damages for humiliation: In the event, the plaintiff feels humiliated by the landlord's acts, the court may force the landlord to pay non-economic damages to the plaintiff. The damages may include the cost of moving expenses, emotional distress, and attorney's fees.

The landlord may be forced to sell their property and pay a fine for violating fair housing laws: If the landlord is found guilty of violating fair housing laws, they may face an additional penalty in which they must sell their property and pay a fine between $100,000 to $1 million. This penalty will mostly be paid to the tenants.

The courts may issue injunctions against the landlord: Even though the penalty for violating fair housing laws is very severe, some courts may issue injunctions against a landlord who committed the violation. In this instance, the landlord is legally forced to follow all fair housing laws and refrain from using any form of discriminatory tactics in the future.

The Landlord may face jail time: Some states may allow a tenant to file criminal charges against their landlord if they are found guilty of violating fair housing laws. In this case, the landlord may face jail time depending on the laws of that state.

Punitive damages may be imposed: A court may impose punitive damages on the landlord if they are found guilty of violating fair housing laws. The damages may be imposed just to send the message that racial, or any other form of discrimination is unacceptable in our society today.

Chapter 8:

Good House Hygiene

This chapter is all about maintaining the cleanliness and general well-being of your rental property.

Housekeeping companies help properties to maintain a good quality of life so that the rentals are available and satisfying for their tenants. There are many factors that go into ensuring hygiene in a rental property, from having clean corridors to maintaining on-site garbage collection services. The first step in maintaining good house hygiene is to hire a good housekeeping company to handle your property. These companies will be able to create a schedule that allows for regular checks of your rental property. This will help make sure that the cleans are being done as needed and that they are effective.

The Tenant Has a Right to a Safe and Decent Housing

Landlords have the responsibility to maintain their rental property in a clean, safe, and decent condition. A landlord is legally obligated to comply with health and safety laws and regulations.

A landlord has the responsibility to ensure that the rental property complies with all local, state, and federal laws and regulations. Some of these laws include:

The warranty of habitability

The implied warranty of habitability is a concept that requires a landlord to provide safe and decent housing.

The warranty of habitability is implied by law and requires the landlord or property manager to maintain the rental unit in such a way that it is fit for human habitation.

When an issue arises with your rental property, it is best to quickly identify the source of the problem.

Oftentimes, tenants will come up with their own ways to fix the problem themselves. This can lead to even more problems down the road. The best idea is to get in contact with your landlord or property manager and let them know what the problem is and how you would like it fixed.

If a tenant fails to alert their landlord of a problem with the rental property, this does not waive any of their rights under the warranty of habitability. The landlord is still obligated to take care of any issues that may be pending.

Local Property maintenance code: Many cities and towns have their own property maintenance codes. These codes can vary from city to city, but the main idea is for tenants to be protected from unsafe rental units. Under these codes, landlords have the responsibility to secure all building areas, maintain inoperable equipment and provide needed services such as heat or running water. In some cases, your local housing authority will inspect your rental property and issue a notice of violation if they find any problem that needs to be fixed by the landlord. Most cities and towns have their own health and safety laws and regulations that tenants and landlords must follow. This includes any unsafe or hazardous rental units that do not comply with the city or town's standards. If there is such a problem with your rental unit, you should contact your local housing authority or landlord right away to get the issue fixed.

Heat requirements: During the winter months, most landlords require tenants to provide their own heat. Under some provisions of state law, a landlord must install heat in a rental unit when it is delivered on or after July 1 of the year in which the tenant moved into a unit. Failure to provide heat can lead to a number of problems. Things like mold, mildew, and condensation can be seen throughout the year if there is no heat source in the unit. If you are living in a rental unit without heating or cooling, it is best that you find out what kind of heating source your landlord has installed. Also, it may be necessary for you to contact your landlord or property manager and find out how long they plan on maintaining the heat source in your rental unit.

Lead Paint and Lead Poisoning: Tenants may be unaware of the problems caused by lead connected to homes or rental units. Untreated lead paint in older homes can cause serious health concerns and even lead poisoning. Some of these issues can be repaired, and others cannot. When it comes to lead paint, landlords are responsible for ensuring a safe environment for tenants.

Lead paint and lead poisoning are both serious issues that should be addressed by owners immediately. If you suspect that your landlord is not making the proper maintenance or repairs to the property, you have a legal right to inquire about the unit's past history of lead poisoning or lead paint. Lead is also dangerous for children, especially those under the age of 6. It is important to test all children for lead poisoning. A doctor can perform a simple blood test that checks the level of lead in the child's blood. If you suspect that the child is being exposed to lead paint or lead-tainted dust, you should immediately contact your local health department and file a complaint regarding the problem.

Have Good Pest Control: Pest control refers to practices or methods used to manage pests. The fundamental goal of pest management is pest prevention and the use of integrated pest management techniques to reduce long-term damage. While it is important for homeowners to take steps toward controlling pests in their respective properties, it can be difficult, expensive, and even impossible at times. This is due to the fact that, in some cases, the pests can cause damage to your property and also pose a threat to your health, which makes it necessary for you to take steps toward controlling them.

Action to Take When a Tenant Reports Pests

There are several basic steps a landlord can take when a tenant reports the presence of pests in their rental unit:

Check the Lease Agreement: The first step, which is crucial and should be done immediately after the tenant has reported a pest problem, is to check the lease agreement on your property. In most cases, you will have a clause stating that if there is a pest infestation in your rental unit, the landlord is required to disclose this information to the tenant without fail. You should check whether there are any other actions or clauses within the contract stating whatever measures you need to take or not take towards resolving this matter. If there is no clause in the lease agreement stating what measures must be taken to resolve an infestation, then when a tenant complains of pests in their rental unit, they can approach the landlord and state that they are doing this because the landlord has failed to take adequate measures to protect their property and health.

Document the Cause: The next thing to do, which is also very important, is to determine what the cause of the infestation is. Most of the time, a source of food will be found. The source could be something that was brought into the home by a tenant, or it could be a food source that has grown in size or been left behind by other pests.

However, in some cases, it may be necessary to find other factors that can lead to the presence of pests, such as the accumulation of garbage or certain pesticides or sprays.

As soon as you are able to determine what is causing the issue, you should take steps toward resolving it by removing any food sources and cleaning up any garbage and rubbish in the home.

Thorough Pest Inspection: The next thing to do is to hire a professional pest inspector that will work with you to resolve this problem from the source. A thorough inspection must be done as soon as possible to find all of the entry points where pests are likely to enter a home. In situations like this, there is usually only one entry point for a large number of pests to enter. The inspection will help you determine what kind of pests you are dealing with, which makes it possible for pest control professionals to use the best equipment and products available. Once you have found all the entry points and have taken steps toward treating them, it is advisable to install more traps in other areas where pests may be able to get inside your property.

How to Prevent Pests in Property

The only way to prevent pests from entering a property is for the tenants and homeowners to be diligent in taking care of their properties. There are various things you can take to prevent undesirable pests from infesting your property.

Follow Proper Cleaning Procedures: It is important for you to follow a process before you clean up the area of your home which is going to be infested with the pest, which will make it less likely that they will get inside.

You should start by thoroughly cleaning the area where the infestation was spotted and then follow a process where you will clean all of the areas that have been cleaned. You should use pesticides in no more than one dose and make sure they are used in a way that is effective. Make certain that all of your floors, walls, and furniture have been thoroughly cleaned.

Keep Trash Clean: Pest control services are typically more expensive than other services, which makes them hard to afford for most tenants. This can make it difficult for a tenant to take care of the problem on their own. That is why it is important for you to keep your home clean and organized, which will help you effectively dispose of the trash and waste that collects on your property, which will reduce a possible source of food for pests. You should also use closed-off spaces as much as possible so that pests can't enter through air vents or gaps in doors and windows. A key factor to look into when it comes to pest control services is the strength of the treatment. You may have seen insect-killing products in the past, but these products often contain harmful chemicals that may be harmful to your health. These chemicals can also harm other pests, so it is highly recommended that you make sure that applications are made properly and in a way that will eliminate any possible threats to the environment.

Educate Tenants on Pest Prevention: It is also important to educate your tenants on proper pest prevention methods. You should make sure your tenants know the main points you have mentioned above and encourage them to take effective steps toward preventing pests from entering their property. It is best to educate tenants before they move in that you will not be providing this type of service, so they should be responsible for the safety of their property. Educating tenants on how to spot signs of infestation and how to prevent this from happening is one way to help them avoid these problems, which will make it less likely for your property to become infested with pests. You can also provide tenants with an in-house guide that gives them a checklist of things they should do when they first move into their apartment. They should also be provided with the number of a local pest control service, which will help them avoid infestations.

Seal the Property: It is possible that there are holes and gaps in the walls of your property where pests could get into your home. This is why you should make sure that the bug walls are sealed to prevent pests from entering your property. You can either use an adhesive patch or a paint sealant to effectively seal the area of the wall. You can also use caulking to seal around the edges of your doors and windows.

Importance of Rental Inspections

A landlord's job is to be a good steward of their rented property, and that includes performing regular inspections. It's common sense, really. Don't you want to know what the condition of your home and property is at any given moment? The following are the benefits of regular rental inspections by landlords:

Inspections ensure that repairs are made as soon as possible: Landlords need to regularly inspect their property in order to identify the necessary repairs and replacements that need to be made. It is important to make these repairs in a timely manner so as to prevent inconveniencing the tenants in any way. Landlords need to keep their rental properties in tip-top shape for inspections and for showings. Don't let your property go to waste by neglecting it or be the cause of a potential tenant walking away from their home because of clutter and disrepair.

Helps avoid problems with insurance companies: Property insurance comes with its own problems, and one of them is the fact that this coverage only pays if there are no issues with the property that can cause damage. If there are minor issues that need to be raised, it is possible for the tenant to claim that they should have been caught prior to the expiration of their coverage on their policy.

Insurance companies will refuse to pay claims if the property is in poor condition or if you have allowed conditions to deteriorate over time. This can also lead to higher premiums, so it's better to nip these issues in the bud with regular inspections.

Prevents deterioration of property and assets: It's never too early to check out the condition of your property, especially if it's still new. Rental inspection reports can be used as a way to plan future improvements and repairs that need to be made in order for the property to achieve its maximum potential. Imagine if you don't discover the mold in your bathroom until several years later. Inspections can also be used to keep track of the overall condition of your home and property so that minor problems before they get worse. Failing to do so and simply assuming that everything's okay with your property is a big risk. Keep a close watch on the condition of your property, and you'll be able to catch on to any potential problems before they start.

Actively prevents loss of property value and any liability issues: Many potential tenants are terrified by the potential of having a problem while they're renting. They need to know that they feel safe and secure in their home, and you can take comfort in knowing that this is something you have control over. You can also reassure them by looking at your property with a fresh set of eyes and making sure everything's above board. Inspections give you the opportunity to hold tenants accountable for the condition of their unit. This can be done through the use of a proper lease clause that designates tenants to take care of and maintain their units in a certain way. Take note, however, that you need to balance this with certain legal realities. A tenant should still have some leeway as to how they use their rental unit. They deserve to have some peace and quiet in their home without turning it into a pigsty.

Prevents undesirable behavior: By regularly inspecting your property, you can quickly discover any problems with the neighbors or other residents. This means that you can quickly address any issues and prevent problems from arising in the future. In this way, you can keep your property from being sued for nuisance and other related reasons. Don't let your tenants' activities outside of their unit negatively impact your property's image.

Determines if the insurance needs to be updated: An annual rental inspection report can help you determine if your insurance needs to be updated and on which areas of your property. This is something that you need to stay abreast of, as there are many factors that can cause your insurance to go up. In some instances, it may not be needed at all, while in other situations, your policy may require coverage on certain sections of your property.

You'll need to take note of the areas that require coverage upgrades. This will save you time and effort during the renewal process for your insurance policies.

It's an opportunity to build a better relationship: In many cases, landlords tend to be absent from their properties, making it difficult for them to get a feel of how their tenants are living in the property. There's nothing wrong with this. Landlords should have lives too. That said, it is still part of a landlord's responsibility to check up on their property and make sure that everything's in order, even if not all the time. Regular rental inspections allow you to maintain a good line of communication with your tenants and make certain that they're taking care of their rental unit properly. It's also a great opportunity to strengthen your relationship with the tenants and come up with methods to make your property even better.

Helps avoid legal liability: Laws are constantly changing, and there are many legal liabilities that can come up when it comes to renting properties. When you get caught by surprise, it's easy to react inappropriately, leading to more trouble in the long run. With rental inspections, you have a better chance of identifying and mitigating these risks right away. When it comes to property management, you can never be too cautious.

Having regular inspections will help you avoid a lot of confusion, stress, and ultimately legal fees.

Helps prevent bad tenants: Just because someone has the money to pay rent doesn't mean they're financially stable enough to do so. Many landlords make the error of selecting renters solely on the basis of their financial ability to pay, ignoring a wealth of information that could assist them in making better decisions. With rental inspections, you get a chance to find out more about your tenant and how they manage their finances. This helps weed out certain people with poor financial habits and poor prospects for paying rent on time each month.

Helps you prevent disputes: Disputes are a fact of life with rentals, and if you're not careful, they'll constantly be the source of stress and frustration. You can avoid this by having rental inspections regularly. By figuring out the condition of your property at any given moment, you can also stop these problems before they get out of hand. The inspection report also acts as a way to resolve potential issues over who's responsible for certain things such as leaking pipes or broken air conditioning.

Helps with claims: Because there are many housing issues such as leaky pipes that occur over time, there is potential for tenants to sue landlords for damages on their rental property. This can be avoided if you have regular inspections and make sure that everything's okay before it ceases being okay. With the proper inspection report, you'll be able to take care of any potential issues with your rental property and prevent them from leading to unnecessary legal fees.

Helps with evictions: Evictions can be a complicated and emotional thing to go through. The process of getting an eviction can be expensive, and even if no one's being evicted, it is likely that some people will find themselves in this situation just through the grace of God. There is always a way to defend yourself against an eviction notice, but that takes time and money. By taking the time to have regular inspections of your property, you can make sure no legal tenant has any room to challenge your right to evict them.

Helps protect your investment: Landlords are always worried about what they spent on the property and how much it will be in the end, no matter how much they paid for it. After all, that's what they put their money into—the rental property—and they don't want to lose out on their investment. With regular inspections and documentation of any issues, you can make sure there's nothing that can come back and bite you in the ass and make you regret putting your money into a long-term investment when it doesn't have to be that way.

Inspections give tenants confidence in their landlord: I'm leaving it up to tenants to find out if their landlord is a good one or not, but rental inspections play an important role in determining how tenants perceive their landlords. A lot of bad landlords will market themselves as a safe bet and lure naïve tenants into dealing with them without doing a background check. If there are any problems with the property, they will then find ways to get their tenants to take responsibility for them and create issues like disputes or evictions. This is where the importance of regular inspections comes in. By making sure that the property is in good condition before letting anyone move into it, and even during the tenancy period, tenants feel comfortable and are convinced that their landlord is responsible and cares for their needs.

Why is a security deposit so important?

The tenant security deposit can be very useful in many cases to the landlord or homeowner. The following are some of the reasons why it is important for a landlord to keep a security deposit:

Damage to property: In the event of a tenant damaging the property that they are renting; it is important for the landlord to have a deposit. This is because the landlord will not be able to recover the money from the tenant if they do not have a security deposit. In this case, the landlord must contact legal experts and insurance companies to protect their rights. The landlord should also contact the tenant and give them a chance to pay for any damages before taking any legal action against them.

Cleaning costs: Sometimes, the landlord may need to pay for cleaning services after the tenant has left the property. This could be as a result of damages to the property that are visible, or it could be because of damage that is not visible. If there is no security deposit, then the landlord will have to cover this cost out of his own pocket. If the tenant moves out and leaves trash or furniture that will need to be removed by paying for such services, the landlord will incur cleaning costs which could be offset by a security deposit if it is there in the first place.

Nonpayment of Rent: A landlord is legally allowed to keep part or the whole amount of the security deposit to cover unpaid rent. The landlord should still give the tenant a chance to come up with the rent, and if they fail, then he will be able to use part or the whole of the deposit to cover for unpaid rent.

Unpaid Bills: A landlord can also use a security deposit to cover unpaid bills from the tenant, such as the electricity bill and the water bill. However, it is not advisable for a landlord to use part or whole of the money as a means of covering unpaid bills on their property. If a tenant moves out of a rental property, the security deposit can be used to pay off any outstanding expenses from the prior tenant.

Contract Breach: The landlord has the right to retain the security deposit if the tenant breaches the lease.

However, in most cases, the tenant is usually asked to provide evidence of damage before a financial claim can take place. A landlord should also explain what they need in order to prove that there has been damage. All this depends on the terms of the lease agreement. The landlord should take care to comply with the state laws when it comes to security deposits. If there are any violations of these laws, the tenant will be able to sue the landlord for damages and also get their deposit back.

Chapter 9:

Working With Contractors

A contractor is someone who does work for others and usually does not provide them with any of the workers necessary for the project. Contractors are usually hired by individuals or companies that are called "prime contractors." A contractor has to follow the instructions of his or her prime contractor. Prime contractors can be government agencies, lumber yards, construction companies, schools, and many more entities.

A common example of a contractor would be a painter who's hired by a customer to paint their house, for example. Another example of a contractor would be the manager of an automotive repair shop who hires an auto mechanic to fix their customers' cars.

What makes someone a contractor is usually determined by the specific laws within their state. For example, in some states, contractors are only allowed to work for certain entities (such as homeowners associations) and only in certain areas (such as alleys), while in other states, there are no such restrictions, and anyone can be a contractor.

Difference Between Licensed and Unlicensed Contractors

As a landlord, you're faced with many decisions when it comes to home renovations. One of the most important selections is whether or not to hire an unlicensed contractor or a licensed contractor. The answer might seem simple because it's just one decision, but there are actually many factors that come into play that make it more complicated than you might expect.

A licensed contractor is a state-certified individual who possesses the necessary skills, knowledge, and abilities to perform certain tasks. These certifications are given to contractors by their state's licensing boards. To acquire one, you must first go through an apprenticeship program and/or schooling in order to graduate with a degree that corresponds with the type of work you want to do. The person must pass the required examination as well as fulfill any other requirements set forth by his or her state. Examples of tasks that require licensing include carpenters, plumbers, and electricians.

Licensed contractors are held to a set of standards that must be adhered to. They must operate within the law and can only use the tools and materials necessary for the job they're performing. They also cannot hire employees who haven't received training if they are going to be employed in certain roles, such as project managers, supervisors, or foremen. The standards are designed to protect the public from harm and to ensure that every individual entering a licensed contractor's workplace is aware of the job they're doing and the materials used.

The quality of the work performed is also important. When you use a licensed contractor, you get a guarantee that they will perform the task appropriately as it was designed. If the work is being done by a licensed contractor, they'll have carried out a blueprint or plan, which will leave your home looking professional and well maintained.

A licensed contractor is experienced in working within set confines, so they can help alert you to any potential problems with your structure or building regulation compliance. They will always be aware of the current rules and regulations that are in place and what could potentially cause problems.

An unlicensed contractor is someone who has not been certified by their state to perform certain tasks. They must still abide by federal and local laws but aren't held to any specific standards. An unlicensed contractor can use any tools or materials deemed suitable for the task at hand. For example, an unlicensed plumber could perform a job by using scrounged metals and construction materials that have been discarded without issue.

Though not all unlicensed contractors are bad people, it's important to recognize that their lack of certification can put you and your property at risk. For example, they do not have any knowledge of the issues that arise from certain materials being used; they could accidentally cut through pipes or create a fire hazard in your home. They also do not have to apply for permits and aren't held to any specific regulations. This means they can bring in unlicensed or undocumented workers to complete the labor, which can result in a lower quality of work and a lack of safety precautions being taken.

The majority of unlicensed contractors who perform remodeling jobs use lower-quality materials and equipment, which affects the overall appearance of your home. They also don't typically have experience with following plans, so they might miss necessary steps that lead to mistakes or other problems with their work.

There are definitely some contractors who aren't worth your time and money and may even be fraudulent. Here are the most common signs that a contractor is unlicensed:

It's unclear whether or not they're certified. If you can't find information about their certification either online or in your state's database, it's probably best to avoid them. They will have no way of proving that they can legally operate in your state.

They ride on a truck that doesn't have any license plate or current registration. If they're not using their own equipment, this could indicate that they don't own their truck and are likely to operate illegally. This can also be a major red flag because if you truly intend to do business with someone, you should make sure that they're abiding by the law and licensed.

They make outrageous claims about the services they provide on their websites or in job descriptions. If there's nothing but great service and high-quality work, then it's likely a scam.

You've never heard of them before, and they don't have any reviews. If you can't find anything about their business, this is a red flag. Ask other businesses whether they are aware of who they are and what they do. If not, you might want to reconsider hiring them to do the job because their lack of experience could indicate that their work won't be up to par.

They won't provide references. If a contractor has worked for a number of people in the past, they should be able to tell you about their clients and how the business relationship went. If they can't provide information about the people they've done work for, then it's best to move on because it means they're not being honest.

What to do When Your Contractor Gives You Problems

Being a landlord can be difficult. There are many aspects of the job that require attention, and one of them is dealing with contractors. When you have a contractor for your rental property, it all comes down to their work and how well they do it. If the contractor does a good job, the landlord will be happy. If the landlord has problems with their contractor, there are things that the landlord can do about it.

When you have a contractor that is performing poorly, you should always remember that you are responsible for them. You will find yourself having to deal with contractors on a daily basis. Many landlords try to abandon their contractors because they do not want to be bothered by them. This is never a good idea. The following is a guideline on what to do when a contractor gives you problems:

Holding back their payment: One of the things that you can do when you have a contractor who gives you trouble is to hold back their payment. Holding back the payment means that you do not have to pay the entire amount right away. You can pay a percentage of their job and then pay the rest at a later date. The contractor strives to satisfy you so that they can receive the remaining portion of their payment in good time. Contractors are often paid once they finish a portion of the job. The contractor is paid a percentage of their job, and the rest of it is paid once the job is completed. The contractor gets most of their payment before they stop working. This will force them to continue with the work. For example, if a contractor has been working for three months but has not yet finished their job, you can pay them 50% of their job and hold back the rest.

Communicate in Writing: Another thing a landlord can do when a contractor gives them trouble is to communicate with them in writing. Communication with a contractor is stronger when something is put in writing. If you have a written agreement, you have no room for error. It is also easier to prove something is true if it has been put on paper. Writing things down will bring the situation to their attention and make them more serious about it.

Send them a text message as well because many contractors often respond better to texts than they do to emails or phone calls. You should also let them know that you are not happy with their performance. Do not be afraid to talk with your contractor. This is a difficult thing to do if you are a landlord, but it is necessary.

Try to understand their point of view: This is going to be the toughest point that a landlord could make. They have to understand why the contractor is doing things incorrectly or not doing things as per the terms of the contract. The best thing that you can do is to talk with their contractor and try to understand why they may be giving you trouble. Sometimes it can be because of your lack of communication; sometimes, it can be because of the quality of their work. If you cannot understand this, then maybe you should reconsider hiring the contractor in the first place. If a contractor is not doing what you want them to do, then it could be best to terminate their contract. Do not let a bad worker affect the quality of your work. The landlord should remember that they are responsible for everything that happens on their property. They should be aware of any problems and address them as quickly as possible. The inspector may be able to offer advice on the situation, such as how the landlord can solve it with their contractor.

Reestablish What the Plan is: Another thing you can do when the contractor is giving you trouble is to reestablish the plan that you had agreed upon. Break down the job into its various parts and discuss what needs to be done by them. Discussing things in further detail will allow your contractor to better understand what is expected of them. Set new timeframes with your contractor. Confirm the conditions under which they will be working and remind them about these conditions.

Check to see what is being done, and check to see if there are any problems.

Refer to the Contract: If you are having problems with your contractor, you should refer to your contract. You will find most of the necessary information here, including the method of payment, how long it should take for completion, and the responsibilities of both parties.

Make sure that all the details of their contract are met by them. If there is something wrong with their work, then you can send them a notice stating that you will be terminating their contract if they do not fix their work.

This will allow you to start again with a new contractor.

Amend the contract: Another thing that you can do is to amend your contract with your contractor. Every problem in your rental property can be addressed in this way. Make sure that you are both on the same page and are aware of what needs to be done. Bring the contract up to date instead of just letting it sit there and collecting dust. Amending the contract gives both the contractor and landlords new terms to work with. If the contract does not allow for the contractor to do certain things, you can amend it to reflect those changes in your rental property.

Escalation: Sometimes, your contractor will take things too far. It may be appropriate to escalate the issue if this occurs. Escalation can be done by threatening to give bad reviews online. This can paint a bad image of their services and will give them a shortage of potential clients who want to hire their services. Since contractors wouldn't want this, they will try their best to be on your good side and perform their job in the best way they can. The problems you were experiencing with them will reduce significantly or completely disappear.

Some Tips on Dealing With Contractors

Contractors are a great way to save money on home improvements, but they can also be a headache! Below are some tips for dealing with contractors once hired.

Understand that not all contractors are shady: Most contractors are honest and will give you a good deal if you play it smart. However, if you hear a lot of bad things about your contractor from other people who were not happy with their experience, it is a good idea to choose someone else to work with. Also, remember that a contract with your contractor should be an itemized list of jobs and their individual costs. If some fees are not clearly designated in the contract, do not pay for them. However, if you choose to get an independent home inspection on the work that is being done on your house from a contracting company, then you can sleep easy knowing that the inspector will look over everything and make sure no mistakes happen. Some companies offer an inspection service with or without a warranty on their work.

Know that your job may cost more than you expect: It is hard to know what a job will cost until you have seen the work, the pricing, and any add-on fees. At times, the cost of doing the job may exceed your expected budget. If you get one bid from someone and then another from someone else, and they are several thousand dollars apart, make sure you ask why this is the case. Some contractors charge more than others because they offer better services and products than other contractors.

If your contractor cannot give you a reason for the difference in price, contact someone else: It is also important to understand the difference between a good contractor and a bad contractor. A good contractor should give you all of the information on how much any costs, who is getting what, how much of it will be paid by who, and when you will receive all of it. A bad contractor might charge you thousands of dollars for doing very little work.

Be prepared for delays: Contractors are sometimes late in getting to the job site and completing it. If you are unprepared for this situation, you may get angry, which is never a good thing. In order to ensure that everything goes smoothly and there is no additional stress, make sure you clear your schedule. It is also good to anticipate such delays when working with contractors to avoid disagreements. Understand that it is natural to have delays at times. We are all human, after all, and no one can be expected to be perfect.

Research on contractors before hiring them: It is wise to take the time to learn as much as you can about different contractors and their experience. This will make an expert decision on which one to hire. Check out some of the recommendations on your town's business license board and check online at sites like online city directories and local phone book sites. Also, consider other reviews on the Internet.

Negotiate with your contractor: It is always a good idea to negotiate with your contractor. It is important to understand what the cost will be, how much of it will be paid by who, and when you will receive the money.

Negotiate with your contractor from the beginning on these points, and make sure you get a hold of them if there are any changes to the contract after it is written up. If you do not know how to negotiate or even where to begin, you can find plenty of information on the Internet for free.

There are also services that will help you with negotiations when it comes to home construction. These services are available for a price, but the results will be worth it. You should also ask your contractor about warranties, guarantees, and any maintenance programs that they offer.

How to Find Reliable Contractors

One of the biggest problems that landlords face is finding reliable contractors. Of course, it's not just a luxury to hire good companies; sometimes, it's the right decision for your property too. There are lots of great ways for landlords to find consistently good contractors, whether by phone or online. This section offers some tips on how landlords can find good contractors.

Start with a plan: Before you even call a contractor, get a plan down of what you want to be done. This is the first step to help you figure out if the contractor is right for the job. If you know exactly what needs to be done and how long it's going to take, it makes the process much easier. The first person who starts talking about "what if" or "how should we do it" is probably not the contractor for your job. If they can't respond right away, they probably don't have the requisite experience to complete the job correctly.

Friends & Family: If you already know a good contractor who has done work for your friends or family, ask them for a recommendation. This is the easiest way to find a good contractor; if people you trust say that a company is good, then it's likely that you'll be satisfied too. If no one knows anyone offhand, it doesn't mean you should give up looking. Local hardware stores employees may also be able to offer valuable information on good contractors because they most likely have worked with them.

Interview at least five contractors: It's a good idea to interview at least five different contractors. You may then compare their rates and services to choose the one that best suits your requirements. You'll also get a feel for what the contractor is like when you meet with them in person; this helps you weed out the inexperienced companies who aren't doing anything wrong; they just don't have a lot of experience under their belt.

Landlord Resources Help You Find Contractors: There is a great resource out there specifically designed to help landlords find reliable contractors. The service, called Need A Pro, gives you the ability to search their database of contractors in your area. Each contractor has a profile that includes reviews from previous customers and pictures of past jobs. You will have access to information about the budget and timeline so that you can get a better idea of what kind of contractor you are dealing with before the quote. The site includes a guarantee, so if you're not satisfied with the results of your first ten quotes, they'll help you find ten more contractors to choose from! If you're looking for a contractor, this is a great place to start.

Ask what work will be done by sub-contractors: As mentioned before, if a contractor isn't able to give you an exact breakdown of the work that will be done by other companies, they're probably not a good choice. If they do offer sub-contractors, that means they will subcontract out some of the work to someone else. This means you can hire different companies to do different parts of the project, but you could end up paying more than you should be paying overall. You want to be sure your contractor is going to do all the work themselves so that they can give you an exact price and timeline. If they are not in a position to handle all the work themselves, then it is a good idea that they inform you about what they won't be able to do.

Check licenses and complaints: Most states require contractors to be licensed. You can do some research online to check if a contractor is licensed in your state. Though this isn't the same as an endorsement from your state licensing agency, you can at least be sure that they're operating with the proper documents. If a company has been fined or has complaints filed against them, it's best to look elsewhere for a contractor.

Endorsements: You can also find out if a contractor has been endorsed by your state by looking to see if there is an organization just for contractors. In some states, you'll be able to find all of the contractors licensed in that area through a website called Contractor's Network. It is available on the internet and provides you with information about contractors in your area. You can then go to the state licensing division's website and look up those businesses that have been approved for endorsements by the state for work with their specific enterprise.

Another way to check a contractor's background is to look online at their online profile. You can find information about the company about how long they've been in business, where they provide services, and reviews of previous customers. By doing a company search on Google, you will be able to find out more information, such as their annual revenue and the year they started offering services in your area. This way, you'll have some hard data and evidence of their reliability before hiring them. You can also read reviews about previous customers who have hired the company for their services, or you can ask friends who have hired a company before for recommendations.

Learn How to Screen Your Contractors

When you are searching for a contractor, it's always nice to know that you are working with someone who will show up on time, complete the project with good quality and results, and communicate often. There are many things to watch out for when selecting your contractors.

This section offers some tips on how to screen your contractors to ensure you are working with the right person.

Pre-screen contractors on the phone and in person: The first step in screening contractors is talking with them on the phone or meeting with them in person. Either way, it will allow you to get a feel for your potential contractors. You will also be able to get an impression of whether they are up to the task through this first contact you have with them. Some important questions to ask them during this first stage are things like how long they have been in this line of work, what tasks they are really good at, how busy they are, how many employees work for them, and so on.

Google the Contractor: Once you find a few potential contractors, the next step is to do some research on them. Do they have a website? If so, log into it and look around. Also, are they a member of any associations? If so, make sure you look at the site for that organization and see if there are any complaints about them being unresponsive or not working on time. Search for their name and get as many entries in Google as you can.

Remember that not all of these postings will be about terrible experiences, so look for the positive ones as well.

Ask for References: Once you find a few potential contractors, ask them to give you two references from other clients that have been happy with their work. Ask for any issues that their clients may be having with their work and how those were handled. Ask them to pull together a list of all of their clients that they have worked on and write the addresses down so you can give the references a call. Additionally, ask them if they can take a few minutes to write you a list of all of their finished projects or at least the list of their most recently completed projects.

Verify their details: Once you have all of the references lined up, you need to go through them and find out if there are any negative experiences. You may even want to talk to the contractor that referred you to this potential contractor. It is always a good idea to check with previous clients before agreeing to work with a new contractor. If you have doubts about how much experience your contractor has, ask them for proof of their credentials and licenses in order for you to feel comfortable that they are qualified and trustworthy enough.

Hire them for one small task: Once you have chosen a contractor, the next step is to hire them for a small project. This way, you can see firsthand how they work and if they are a trustworthy person. If your project is emotionally charged, such as building a custom home, it may be best to hire someone who has done this before in order for them to be able to handle the pressure and for you not to feel rushed or uncomfortable with potentially not completing the project on time.

Whatever type of project you're working on, being as picky as possible with your contractor choices is always a smart idea. If you find someone that is not trustworthy, then don't work with them. It will save you more stress and time in the long run.

Chapter 10:

The Importance of Good Bookkeeping

Every landlord wants to be organized, not just because it's easier to manage their property and their tenants, but also because they want a more profitable and enjoyable life.

In this chapter, we're going to talk about the importance of being organized as a landlord, how you can get your rental business in order, and the different types of organizing you can do for your rental property.

If you're disorganized or have just been putting off getting organized for your rental property, now is the time to get organized.

To rent your property and advise your tenants are the two things that come first in your list of tasks: they should be done first because if you don't do them, then the other things will fall behind.

Ways Landlords Can Get Their Things Organized

It seems like for many landlords, having the ability to maintain a clean and organized living environment is something that is impossible to find. It's easy for your tenants to get things out of order or mess up your property. But don't fret!

There are ways that you can get your business organized as a landlord, which is explained below:

Organize Your Tasks: The first thing that you should do as a landlord is to organize your tasks. This will make it easier for you to keep track of your work and communicate with your tenants. The first method you can use is by creating a list of tasks. You need to take care of or review this list periodically. You can create these lists on the computer or use paper and pencil. The easier you are able to keep track of your tasks, the better. For example, you can print out a list of all of your household chores or add a checklist to your phone. It is also very important to re-evaluate these tasks occasionally. If there are things that need to be added to your list, then the next step is reevaluation. It's important for you to remember one simple concept - there is no best way for someone else to organize their life for them other than doing it yourself.

Document storage and sharing: This involves the use of online storage facilities to store your documents. Make sure that you stay organized by making sure that you have a system in place so that your building information doesn't get scattered throughout your house.

The online storage system is also important since it makes it easier to retrieve tenant and property documents. Some of the documents that you should have in place are the lease, city and county tax information, and any additional documentation that you need to provide to tenants. Ensure that you have these documents in order so they are easy to find.

Google Calendar Sync: Before you use this software, you should read through the directions in order to make sure that it is set up for your specific needs. A great feature of Google Calendar is that it will sync with your computer and your mobile phones, which makes it easy to plan out your day. Ensure you have a backup in place in case anything happens to your computer or phone. Having a calendar will help you schedule what is going on around the building and in different locations. For example, you can have a calendar for your tenants, one for each tenant, and one for yourself. This will make it easy to communicate and keep track of different events that are happening outside of the building.

Apps and Software That are Useful for Landlords in organizing and Managing Their Rental Properties

Property management can be a hassle for many landlords. Tracking down what has been paid, who is coming and going, coordinating maintenance schedules and tenant bids can consume a lot of time. Many landlords are turning to new app developers to help make the job easier with some awesome property management apps.

Landlords can use a variety of apps and tools to help them

manage their properties. The following is a list of some of the best ones, with their features explained:

Rental Property Manager: This app allows you to manage your tenants, income, and expenses by simply signing into one account. You can use the app to download contracts, track payments, enforce fines for late rent, and much more. It also allows you to instantly send notices via email or text message if there are any problems with repairs or maintenance. It will also give you an automatic tenant rating, so you know if the tenant is reliable or not.

Project Tenant: This app, like the name implies, helps you manage your tenants by providing you with a digital tenant dossier. You can use this software to manage your leases and rental payments easily. It's easy to create schedules for maintenance and watch over all of the tenants you have in one location. The App also allows you to track down who is coming and going from the apartment as well as keep up with inventory.

MyRentalProperty: This app is useful for keeping up with maintenance and tenant payments. You can create a to-do list for each day and also log any ongoing issues or work orders. The app allows you to manage multiple properties from one location, as well as keep up with income, expenses, tenant payments, and maintenance schedules. It also has the ability to keep track of who is entering the property and record notes on each visit. If you want to make your job as a landlord easier, it is strongly advised.

Property Managers App: This app is a good one for managing your properties. It allows you to get up-to-date information on your rent, maintenance, tenant payments, and expenses. You can also create invoices and statements for each month with the information you have verified. It will also keep track of who has entered the property and when.

Smart Tenant App: This app can be used to manage your tenants and keep track of who is coming and going. Users can also use the app to note any problems or maintenance work orders on their own home or anywhere else. The process of filing for termination due to non- payment is a breeze as well with this app.

Maintenance Manager: This app is great to help you organize your maintenance work orders and keep track of who is doing what. It can also help you organize project bids, schedule maintenance, and watch over the progress. It is one of the best tools for landlords as it allows you to manage multiple properties all from one location.

Repair Log: This app allows you to make your work easier by logging any maintenance work orders you might have in a very easy-to-use way. It allows you to take photos of the problem as well and submit them when creating the order. It is a great tool for landlords, as it can help you keep track of who is doing what and when.

Lease Manager: This is an app that can help you manage your lease agreements if there are any problems with them or if anything needs updating. It will also allow you to keep track of lease renewals, late notices, and photographs. To make things easier for landlords, it will allow you to email people directly from the app. If any problems arise, a landlord can report them to the proper authorities quickly and easily.

Make things easier for yourself.

Between the prestige, capital growth, and appreciation potential of rental properties, landlords and investors are becoming more prevalent in every market across the nation. In order to best manage your rental properties efficiently, you need to understand accounting basics.

Accounting refers to the recording or summarizing of financial transactions. The single purpose of bookkeeping is to create an asset and liability account balance sheet, with expenses, income, and cash flows recorded in the appropriate areas. For example, you collect rent from your tenants on a monthly basis. You then record the rent in the debit column of a journal entry account called Rents Expense Account. As a debit to the

Rents Expense Account, you would also record a credit for the same amount under the Collected Rent Receivable Account.

Renting a property should be treated just like any other business or income-generating activity. Every penny should be accounted for and used appropriately. For this to be possible, landlords must understand the basics of accounting.

Rental Property Accounting Basics

The following are some of the basic accounting tips for your rental property explained:

Separate Your Business and Personal Finances: It is important for any landlord to separate their personal account from their business account. You do not want to mix personal and business finances as this can create problems down the road. For example, if your business fails, you do not want to have it affect your personal life. When buying a rental property, separate your bank account from the business account. This would make paying bills very easy because you will only have to pay from one account. Separating these two accounts is also important because it makes things easier with the IRS when reporting taxes.

Consider Having a Separate Account for Each Property: It is also important to consider separating your rental properties into accounts. This allows you to track expenses, income, and cash flow from each property. For example, let's say you own four rental properties and want to track expenses for all of them. Depending on which account you want to use for each rental property, it can be easy to maintain these separate accounts, or it can become a hassle.

If you decide to use the same account for all properties, you need to track expenses and income separately, which is tiresome. The best thing about having separate accounts is that it makes keeping track of cash flow very easy. For example, if one property receives more rent than expected, it shows up in the property's bank account without any problem.

Automate Everything: You should also consider automating everything. This will allow you to create more profit-generating rental property management systems.

For example, a rental property management system can be used to automatically adjust your vacancy rate, the amount of rent you collect per month, and the amount of money that is owed on your mortgage without you having to do any work. You can also automate rent payments. If you have more than one property, one way to do this is to create a multi-property rental payment program. This will allow you to keep track of rent payments and all the related information that is involved with your rental property management. If you opt to use an online rental property management platform, keep in mind that it might be quite costly. Each system varies in price, and some systems can cost thousands of dollars for the software and even more for the installation fees. To obtain the greatest rates and get the most out of your property management program, you must be very attentive and ensure that the installation is done by a reliable company.

Maintain Your Financial Records Properly: The single most important element of accounting for rental property is to maintain your financial records properly. You should record all your expenditures on a monthly basis and then post these expenses as well. This will tell you what you have spent money on since it prevents you from overspending. You should also calculate all your rent payments. If you own multiple properties, you must figure out the average rent for each one. This data will show you how much money is spent on repairs and maintenance for your rental properties, as well as how much is paid on rent.

Know how to classify your income and expenses: When classifying your income and expenses, make sure you do not over classify your expenses. For example, if someone asks you for the depreciation on a computer system that you purchased last year, it will be hard to prove that this was an expense because it wasn't actually purchased last year. You will also have a problem supporting these expenses if they are high because you may classify them inaccurately. It is very important to classify your rental property expenses correctly. If you do not, your financial records will not be able to prove how much money is going towards the repairs and maintenance of your rental property or how much money is actually used for the business.

Balance your checkbook to match transactions: The final key element of basic accounting for rental property is to balance your checkbook. It lets you see at a glance the difference in balances in the different areas of your business. For example, if you have one property with a balance of $200,000 and a second property that has a balance of $100,000, you will know that there is a

$200,000 difference. When balancing your checkbook, it is important to include all the income and expenses in your ledger. This will ensure that you do not leave anything out of the ledger. It is also important to note that it can be easy to miss small transactions, even though they might not seem like much at the time. It is always a good idea to keep a paper trail of your business transactions by printing off everything that has taken place on your computer. Being able to balance a bank statement is also important because it allows you to see how much money you have taken in and how much money you have spent. This allows you to see if there are any problems with either your income or your expenses.

Benefits of Having a Property Manager

A property manager can help with tenant relations, maintenance, rent collections, and outreach to new renters.

Property managers are important for landlords and homeowners who want to ensure their properties are being taken care of without having to do it themselves. This section will mainly focus on understanding why it is important for a landlord to have a property manager.

The advantages of employing a property manager

They can help set the right rental rates: A property manager will get an idea of how to set the right rental rates. They will have an understanding as to what other rentals in the area charge and will be able to determine whether you need to increase or decrease your rates. Many people are unaware that they are charging too little for their rentals, thus leading them to lose out on money. The property manager is able to help determine whether the current prices are correct or not by comparing the rental values of other properties in a similar area.

They can help with tenant relations: A property manager can help with tenant relations. They have the ability to live there and check out the unit, leading them to know what is happening inside of the rental. The property manager will be able to provide a sense of security for both the landlord and tenants. It is through tenant relations that an establishment can get good word-of-mouth from other renters and also retain their quality by only renting out quality rentals that meet their standards.

They can help with maintenance: A property manager has the ability to live there and make sure that the tenants are taking care of the property correctly. Most landlords lack the time or desire to be onsite nearly all of the time to make sure that everything is running smoothly. This can mean problems will go unattended for long periods of time, but with a property manager that is not an issue. They are able to be onsite most of the time, making sure that everything is being taken care of by the tenants.

Collecting and depositing rent payments on time:

The rental property is how most income is generated; thus, it is important to collect the rent payments on time. A lot of people do not realize that this type of job can be handled by a property manager. They are able to collect the payment and deposit them right into an account on time. A property manager will make sure that the rental payments are being deposited into your bank account every month. They will be able to conduct any necessary banking transactions to ensure that it gets done correctly and on time.

They can help with marketing: A property manager will be able to assist in marketing. They will also use their connections to network with other renters and homeowners. They are able to find out who is looking to rent a unit, what kind of rates they are looking for, and how much they are willing to pay. They can compile this information into a report that can be presented when showing the rental units to potential renters.

Finding the Right Tenants: A property manager can help with finding the right tenants. They will be able to find out what kind of people are looking for rentals, what their requirements are, and how much they are willing to pay. A property manager is able to know what other landlords and homeowners are charging for their properties and compare it to your rental. By knowing the type of people that you want as tenants, you can make sure that they have the best chance of choosing your rental over any other similar listings.

Ensuring you comply with property regulations: The property manager is able to ensure that the rental complies with all of the property regulations. They are able to make sure that there are no environmental issues and that no laws or ordinances are being broken. The property manager will be able to check for all of the building permits and other documents required by local authorities and make sure they are being followed.

Knowing what ordinances or codes a rental is subject can help in making sure it meets your required standards.

Ensuring you comply with any contracts: All of the agreements that are signed by both you and the property manager will be able to be enforced. This means that some companies are not able to service their clients correctly. All contracts will have to be complied with and followed in order for them to be enforced. As a landlord, you have made a contract with the tenants when they are renting from you; thus, it is important for them to follow it. You have also made contracts with yourself when agreeing on the rental rates, rules and regulations, and amenities that you want to be provided. A property manager can help enforce these contracts by making sure they are being followed.

Maximizing Profitability of Your Property: A property manager is able to maximize the profitability of your rental property. They are able to market your rental correctly and increase its value by helping with tenant relations and finding the right renters. By having a good marketing plan, you can make sure that you will be able to get a return on your investment as well as have a good return of investment.

Having good tenant relations will help ensure that there are fewer problems in the future. Finding the right tenants is also important as they will be more likely to pay their rent on time, stay and continue renting from you, and leave positive reviews. By having a property manager, you can increase the profitability of your rental property and make a good return on your investment.

How to Find a Good Property Manager

Locating a suitable property manager is one of the most important and difficult tasks when you are starting out to buy a new home. Here are some suggestions for finding excellent property management:

Get referrals: You can begin your search for a property manager by asking friends and family for recommendations. Again, you might as well just ask everyone you know where they have found a good property manager and why they chose them. Remember that not everyone has great things to say about each property manager, but the ones who do will probably be your starting point when looking for a property manager.

Do a little detective work: Nothing is worse than finding a property manager who isn't delivering what they've promised, but you won't find out unless you ask them directly. Conduct a little research to see if they have a good reputation. Google their name along with words like 'negative,' 'reviews,' and 'complaints.' Keep in mind that not every property manager is going to have complaints filed against them, but you'll probably find a few that stand out.

Interview Candidates: It is important to interview your potential candidates. Explain what you expect a property manager to do for you, and then ask them how they intend on going about doing it. Pay attention to what they're saying and keep an eye out for any hollow promises or unrealistic ambitions. Be sure not to settle for anyone who claims that they can do more than is possible.

Take your time: Asking someone to manage your home is not an easy task, so allow your potential candidates enough time to complete the application process. It is best if you can get them to provide references, so make sure you ask for their character references and contact the people who put them in this position in the first place.

Keep an eye on things: Finally, once you've selected a property manager and you're ready to sign a contract with them, make sure that you review it

carefully. Remember that once you've signed with a property manager, they become responsible for renting out your home or finding potential buyers.

Conclusion

By now, I hope you're ready to jump into rental real estate with both feet. As you've seen throughout the book, although you do need to do a lot of research to find the right properties, investing in rentals is pretty straightforward as long as you understand what you're doing. Doing your investigation is the key to finding the right property. Not only do you need to understand the real estate market in the area, but you also need to review the property itself.

A lot of information has been offered in this book, but the key element is ensuring you get the right tenants and doing whatever it takes to have a good relationship with them. It will make your job as a landlord or homeowner easier and less stressful.

Understanding housing regulations and fair housing are also key components to avoiding incurring losses due to being sued and having to pay for damages. Treating all tenants equally and ensuring that you provide them with the best housing conditions is crucial for any landlord to succeed in this field.

In addition, managing your finances diligently and monitoring your cashflows are also very important for your success.

As seen in the book, this is an important element most landlords ignore. Knowing your numbers determines whether you will grow and at what rate your business will grow.

I hope the tips and information offered in this book will be very helpful to you, whether you are an aspiring landlord or you already own several rental properties. The information offered is also helpful for readers who want to increase their knowledge of managing rental properties. Now that you've gathered all of the necessary tools and skills, it's time to take that first step toward financial freedom.

From Stress to Success: Strategies for Profitable Properties Management

"LARRY HOWTON"

....

Thank you for buying this book.